Table of Contents (Office 365 for small businesses)

CONTENT UPDATES

ExamREVIEW is an independent content developer not associated/affiliated with Microsoft. The exam described is the trademark of Microsoft. We at ExamREVIEW develop study material entirely on our own. Our material is fully copyrighted. Braindump is strictly prohibited. We provide essential knowledge contents, NOT any generalized "study system" kind of "pick-the-right-answer-every time" techniques or "visit this link" referrals.

All orders come with LIFE TIME FREE UPDATES. When you find a newer version of the purchased product all you need to do is to go and download. **Please check our web site regularly.**

http://www.examreview.net/free_updates.htm

About this book

According to MS, there is the Office 365 for small businesses exam coded 74-325 that covers these topics:

Administer Microsoft Office 365

Administer Exchange and Lync Online

Administer SharePoint Online

The Small Business version of Office 365 has relatively less to configure, but you are still expected to know SharePoint, Lync and Exchange. We give you knowledge information relevant to the exam specifications. To be able to succeed in the exam, you'll need to apply your earned knowledge to the question scenarios. Many of the exam questions are written to be less straight forward. They tend to be framed within the context of short scenarios.

The exam is not too difficult. However, Office 365 is constantly evolving so changes to the exam contents may be frequent. Be ready to see conflicting information from different sources everywhere!

This ExamFOCUS book focuses on the more difficult topics that will likely make a difference in exam result. The book is NOT intended to guide you through every single official topic. You should therefore use this book together with other reference books for the best possible preparation outcome.

Preparing for your trial

The best way to learn is to actually go through a trial. MS offers a 30-day free trial in certain plans.

Select an Office 365 plan for business

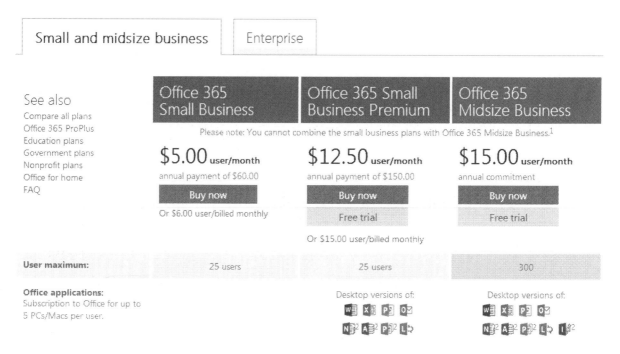

	Office 365 Small Business	Office 365 Small Business Premium	Office 365 Midsize Business
	\$5.00 user/month	\$12.50 user/month	\$15.00 user/month
	annual payment of \$60.00	annual payment of \$150.00	annual commitment
	Buy now	Buy now	Buy now
	Or \$6.00 user/billed monthly	Free trial	Free trial
		Or \$15.00 user/billed monthly	
User maximum:	25 users	25 users	300

See also
Compare all plans
Office 365 ProPlus
Education plans
Government plans
Nonprofit plans
Office for home
FAQ

Please note: You cannot combine the small business plans with Office 365 Midsize Business.[1]

Office applications: Subscription to Office for up to 5 PCs/Macs per user.

For this exam, a small business premium trial with support for 10 users is good enough. You will be allowed to create a new subdomain and user ID while retaining the onmicrosoft.com part.

create your new user ID

* User ID:

michael @ ExamREVIEW .onmicrosoft.com

You'll use this to sign in to Office 365. Can I remove the .onmicrosoft.com part?

your user ID
michael@ExamREVIEW.onmicrosoft.com

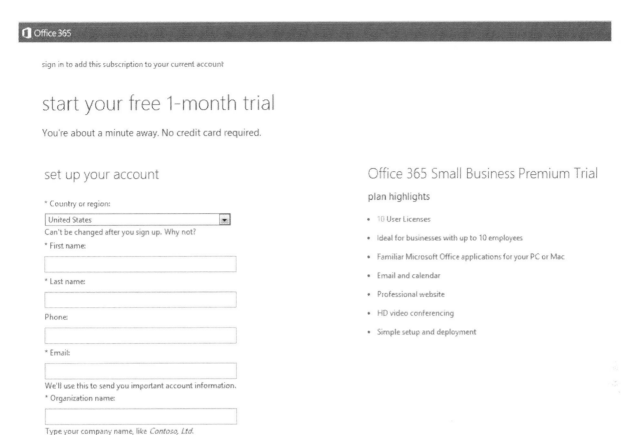

You won't be able to continue unless you can supply a strong password. Refer to the screen capture below for the definition of strong password:

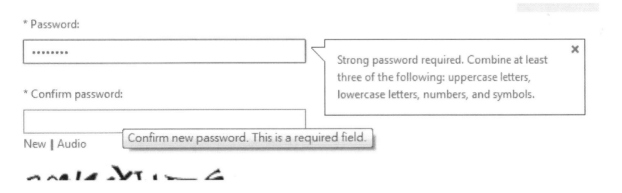

The Office 365 Admin Center is where you perform all the admin duties. Do note that unlike onsite servers, you do not really have much technical stuff to fine tune since the servers are being hosted by MS.

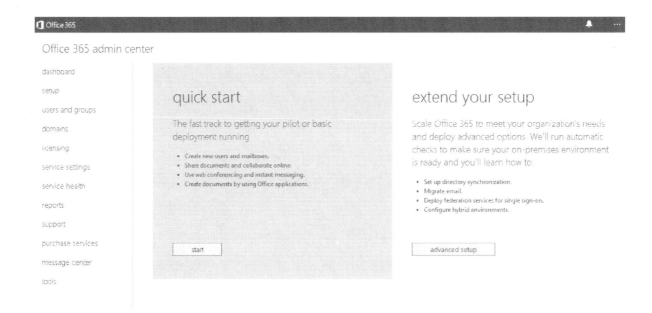

A confirmation email will be sent to you from MS. Do remember, to use Office 365 you need to have a reliable internet connection. And you need a capable browser. In theory you need to use the latest version of IE. In practice, Chrome also works fine.

Welcome to your Microsoft Office 365 Trial

Sign in and get started today!

Sign in

User ID (What is this?)

Name: michael yu
User ID: michael@ExamREVIEW.onmicrosoft.com

During your trial, you'll have the opportunity to try out Microsoft's best communication and collaboration services, all brought together online. Sign in with your User ID to get started setting up and managing your services.

Throughout your trial, we'll send you messages with tips and tricks to help you get the most from Office 365.

GET STARTED WITH YOUR TRIAL

Account Information

Organization name:
ExamREVIEW

Service:
Office 365 Small Business Premium Trial

Trial start date:

You will have 10 licenses to play with for a month.

licenses

subscriptions   purchase services

SUBSCRIPTION	QUANTITY	COST
Office 365 Small Business Premium Trial	10 user licenses	No cost

In terms of system requirement (OS, browser, and Office client), you should refer to this Change Log for the most updated information:

http://community.office365.com/en-us/wikis/manage/office-365-system-requirements-wiki.aspx

Change Log

Product	Description	Effective On
Office 2010	We have released Service Pack 2 for Office 2010. While we recommend immediate deployment of all service packs and public updates, Service Pack 2 is currently only required by 14 October 2014.	14 October 2014
Outlook 2013 and Auto-mapping	REMOVED We are resolving this issue via a server side fix. Client hotfixes are no longer required	n/a
Outlook 2010 and Auto-mapping	REMOVED We are resolving this issue via a server side fix. Client hotfixes are no longer required	n/a
Windows Vista	Office 365 support for Windows Vista now follows its support lifecycle	n/a

Keep in mind, IE is NOT the only browser possible although non-IE browser are mostly being end-of-supported. If you are using IE, IE 8 is probably the minimum. In terms of client OS, Windows XP and Vista are still okay (MS will end support for XP in April 2014 though). In terms of Office client, Office 2007 would require that SP3 be applied. Outlook 2003's status is end-of-support.

Another thing – while Windows Powershell is listed in the exam BOK, MS said that using Windows Powershell to manage Office 365 for small business is NOT recommended:

Feature	Office 365 Small Business	Office 365 Small Business Premium
Administer Office 365 by using the Office 365 admin center	No	No
Administer Office 365 by using the Office 365 portal	Yes	Yes
Manage core service settings from Office 365	Yes	Yes
Use Windows PowerShell to manage Office 365	No[1]	No[1]
Protect content by using Windows Azure AD Rights Management	No	No

Note:

1 Windows PowerShell can be used, but is not recommended.

2 Windows Azure AD Rights Management is not included, but can be purchased as a separate add-on and will enable the sup

3 Windows Azure AD Rights Management is not available with Office 365 Government G3 or Office 365 Government G4.

Note:

1 Windows PowerShell can be used, but is not recommended.

2 Windows Azure AD Rights Management is not included, but car

To find out more on the latest service changes, refer to the message center of the admin portal:

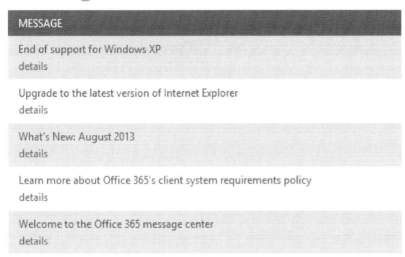

message center

MESSAGE
End of support for Windows XP
details
Upgrade to the latest version of Internet Explorer
details
What's New: August 2013
details
Learn more about Office 365's client system requirements policy
details
Welcome to the Office 365 message center
details

If you click Details, you can further examine the message details.

End of support for Windows XP

details
Microsoft will end all support for Windows XP on 8 April 2014—please upgrade all Windows XP workstations to Windows 8 or Windows 7 prior

While Office 365 will not block connections from fully patched Windows XP computers after 8 April 2014, connectivity to the service will be at r
that have not deployed all service packs and automatic updates run an even higher risk of Office 365 connectivity issues after support for Wind

If you experience a technical problem connecting to Office 365 from a Windows XP machine after 8 April 2014, Microsoft Customer Support an
reproduce the problem on a supported operating system.

Sincerely,
The Office 365 team

additional information

Office 365 for Small Business

Cloud computing and the related technologies

Cloud computing is all about distributed computing. An application is built using resources from multiple services from the same or different locations. By knowing the endpoint to access the services, the user can use software as a service, much like utility computing. Behind the scene there are grids of computers and the user does not need to know the details of the background stuff. No more access to things like server logs, background services …etc! Office 365 is a cloud based solution. To be precise, it is based on Windows Azure. Therefore, topics involving Windows Azure may show up in the exam.

Active Directory AD stores information of all network objects and makes the information easy to find. It is a logical and hierarchical presentation and storage of shared resources such as servers, volumes, printers...etc. Windows Azure is in fact a cloud implementation of AD. Active Directory Certificate Services allows you to create, distribute, and manage customized public key certificates. Active Directory Domain Services are responsible for storing directory data and managing communication between users and domains plus administering user logon processes. Active Directory Federation Services ADFS provides Web single-sign-on SSO for authenticating web user to multiple Web applications.

Windows Intune is a cloud-based client management solution that supports these Windows versions:

- Windows XP Professional with SP3, x86 only

- Windows Vista Enterprise, Ultimate, or Business editions, x86 or x64

- Windows 7 Enterprise, Ultimate, or Professional editions, x86 or x64

- Windows 8 Enterprise or Pro editions, x86 or x64

They must have Windows Installer 3.1 ready, and you must login as a member of the Administrators group on the local computer. To use the web based admin console you need IE 8 or later. Very importantly, port 80 and port 443 must not be blocked by the firewall.

You need to buy the service. After purchase you may use the Windows Intune account portal to manage your Windows Intune subscription. You may also specify those users who can access it. Do note that Windows Intune makes use of the peer distribution platform in Windows 8 Pro/Enterprise, which is the same technology behind BranchCache. BranchCache Distributed Cache mode will be automatically enabled by the Windows Intune client UNLESS there is a group policy that explcitely disables BranchCache. Also note that Windows Intune has a policy management functionality in the Policy workspace which has nothing to do with Group Policy. The two policy management systems are for serving similar purposes but they operate independently. There is a possibility to have policy conflicts!

When you sign into Windows 8 using a MS account known as a Windows Live ID (in fact you can create a MS account that is linked to any email address), Windows 8 can automatically sync most settings other than passwords. In fact, settings sync can be done through the PC settings pane of Change PC Settings. From there you can find an item called Sync Your Settings.

Add a user

What email address would this person like to use to sign in to Windows? (If you know the email address they use to sign in to Microsoft services, enter it here.)

Email address

When you sign in to Windows with a Microsoft account, you can:

- Download apps from Windows Store.
- Get your online content in Microsoft apps automatically.
- Sync settings online to make PCs look and feel the same—this includes settings like browser favorites and history.

There are two options for signing in:

Microsoft account

Signing in to PCs with your email address lets you:

- Download apps from Windows Store.
- Get your online content in Microsoft apps automatically.
- Sync settings online to make PCs look and feel the same—like your browser history, picture, and color.

Local account

Signing in with a local account means:

- You have to create a user name and account for each PC you use.
- You'll need a Microsoft account to download apps, but you can set it up later.
- Your settings won't be synced across the PCs that you use.

Add your Microsoft account

We'll save this info so you can use your account with Mail, Calendar, People and Messaging.

Email address

Password

Sign up for a Microsoft account

A local account is not the same as a MS account. A local account can be used to operate Windows 8, but downloading apps from the app store won't be possible with it. You can always switch between a local account and a MS account from PC settings. You simply need to use the Switch to a local account or Switch to a Microsoft account button located under your username.

ActiveSync is for synchronizing email messages, calendar, and contacts lists in the Exchange Server mailbox with a Windows Mobile powered device (such as Windows Phone). From with the Exchange Control Panel there is an ActiveSync Access tab which allows you to control how your mobile devices may connect to Exchange. You may create a device access rule to determine if a user can synchronize to Exchange with a specific mobile device product model. The rule will be applied to devices that are not covered by any personal exemptions. Direct push is a technology that works by maintaining an open connection between the phone and the server such that new mail items can be automatically pushed to the phone without requiring SMS notification messages.

Single sign-on SSO refers to the kind of access control method which enables a user to authenticate once and gain access to network resources of other software systems. Kerberos is an authentication protocol in use by the newer Windows Servers (since Windows 2000) for facilitating the implementation of SSO.

Deployment readiness

You use the Office 365 Deployment Readiness Tool (OnRamp) to evaluate readiness for Office 365. The link is:

http://community.office365.com/en-us/wikis/manage/535.aspx

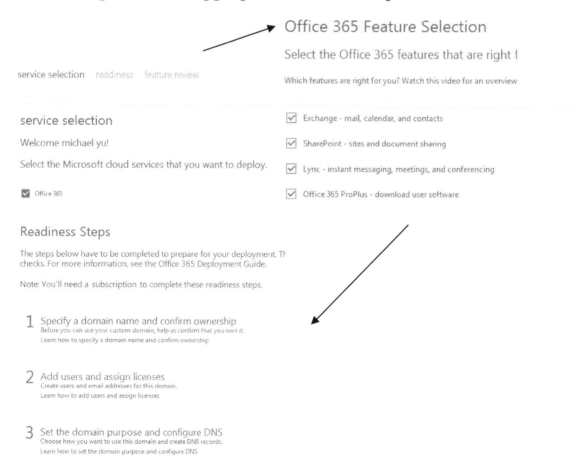

Microsoft Office 365 Deployment Readiness Tool / OnRamp for Office 365

Posted by Office 365 Deployment Guidance and Tools on 4/28/2011 11:17 AM

Microsoft Office 365 Deployment Readiness Tool

The Office 365 Deployment Readiness Tool is now apart of Office 365 Setup and OnRamp for Office 365!

Click here to sign in / sign up and evaluate your readiness for Office 365!

You need to get a free user ID in order to use it. You may then select the features to produce the appropriate readiness steps:

Office 365 Feature Selection

Select the Office 365 features that are right f

Which features are right for you? Watch this video for an overview

service selection   readiness   feature review

service selection

Welcome michael yu!

Select the Microsoft cloud services that you want to deploy.

☑ Office 365

☑ Exchange - mail, calendar, and contacts

☑ SharePoint - sites and document sharing

☑ Lync - instant messaging, meetings, and conferencing

☑ Office 365 ProPlus - download user software

Readiness Steps

The steps below have to be completed to prepare for your deployment. Th checks. For more information, see the Office 365 Deployment Guide.

Note: You'll need a subscription to complete these readiness steps.

1 Specify a domain name and confirm ownership
   Before you can use your custom domain, help us confirm that you own it.
   Learn how to specify a domain name and confirm ownership

2 Add users and assign licenses
   Create users and email addresses for this domain.
   Learn how to add users and assign licenses

3 Set the domain purpose and configure DNS
   Choose how you want to use this domain and create DNS records.
   Learn how to set the domain purpose and configure DNS

Walking through the interfaces

If you log off and logon again, you will see the Windows 8 App style screen (they call it the Office 365 Portal, with the upper part being known as the Getting started pane. According to MS, this pane is available ONLY for the first 30 days):

For exam prep purpose you should go through all the functions of the "Manage your organization" section, which includes service settings, users & groups, licenses, domains, service status, support, website and message center.

Manage your organization

service settings
Manage organization-wide settings

users & groups
Add users, reset passwords, and more

licenses
Manage and purchase licenses

domains
Manage your website and email

service status
Track service health and maintenance

support
Get help and online support

website
Manage your public website

message center
Read and plan for upcoming se changes

Service settings allows you to turn on and turn off individual functions on an organization-wide basis. You do not fine tune the details here. You simply enable and disable them. By default all of them are ON, but you may turn them off selectively. The following screen captures are pretty self explanatory.

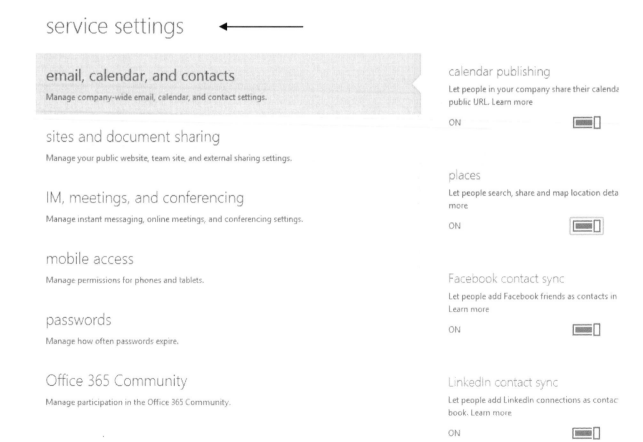

service settings ⟵

email, calendar, and contacts
Manage company-wide email, calendar, and contact settings.

sites and document sharing
Manage your public website, team site, and external sharing settings.

IM, meetings, and conferencing
Manage instant messaging, online meetings, and conferencing settings.

mobile access
Manage permissions for phones and tablets.

passwords
Manage how often passwords expire.

Office 365 Community
Manage participation in the Office 365 Community.

calendar publishing
Let people in your company share their calenda public URL. Learn more
ON

places
Let people search, share and map location deta more
ON

Facebook contact sync
Let people add Facebook friends as contacts in Learn more
ON

LinkedIn contact sync
Let people add LinkedIn connections as contac book. Learn more
ON

tps://portal.microsoftonline.com/ServiceSettings/ExchangeSettingsPro.aspx#

service settings

email, calendar, and contacts
Manage company-wide email, calendar, and contact settings.

sites and document sharing   ⬅——————
Manage your public website, team site, and external sharing settings.

IM, meetings, and conferencing
Manage instant messaging, online meetings, and conferencing settings.

mobile access
Manage permissions for phones and tablets.

passwords
Manage how often passwords expire.

Office 365 Community
Manage participation in the Office 365 Community.

external sharing
Allow external users to access your team site and documents. Learn more

Remove individual external users

site creation
Let people in your company create new sites for managing projects and documents. Learn more

external services
Let people in your company use external services, like Bing Translator, which may not meet all compliance criteria. Learn more

service settings

email, calendar, and contacts
Manage company-wide email, calendar, and contact settings.

sites and document sharing
Manage your public website, team site, and external sharing settings.

IM, meetings, and conferencing   ⬅——————
Manage instant messaging, online meetings, and conferencing settings.

mobile access
Manage permissions for phones and tablets.

passwords
Manage how often passwords expire.

Office 365 Community
Manage participation in the Office 365 Community.

dial-in conferencing
Set up dial-in conferencing so people who don't have Lync can join your meetings by phone. An audio conferencing provider is required. Learn more

Setup

online presence
Decide who can see the online presence of users in your company. Learn more

- ⦿ Everyone in your company
- ◯ Only people on the user's Contacts list

external communication
Let users talk and chat with people outside your company. Learn more

ON

recording
Let people record their audio and video conferences. Learn more

ON

Dial-in conferencing allows phone access to online meetings for those having no access to computer. For this to work there must be an audio conferencing provider offering the necessary dial-in numbers, conference codes, and identification number. Presence statuses may include Available, Busy, Away, and Do Not Disturb. In fact, the status is based on Outlook Calendar or other Lync activities.

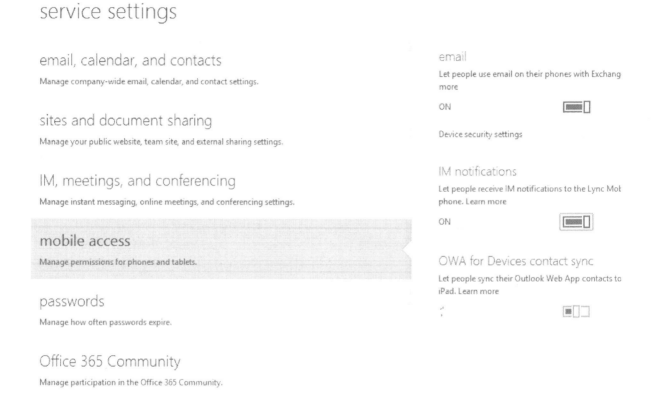

You can access email, conduct instant messaging, and share documents from your mobile devices (phone and tablet...etc). The possible devices include Windows Phone, iPhone, iPad, Android, Symbian, and BlackBerry phones. Ideally your mobile device should be compatible with Exchange ActiveSync. Otherwise you will need to set up POP3/IMAP4 access.

OWA for devices is a feature that supports mobile devices. OWA Outlook Web App is a native app for iPhone and iPad. It allows mobile devices to work and sync with Outlook. Simply put, it works almost the same way that Outlook Web Access does in a PC based browser (and with some additional features). Plans that support this include Office 365 Small Business and Small Business Premium; Office 365 Midsize Business; Office 365 Enterprise E1, E3 and E4; Office 365 Kiosk K1 and K2; Office 365 Education A2, A3 and A4; and other Exchange Online plans.

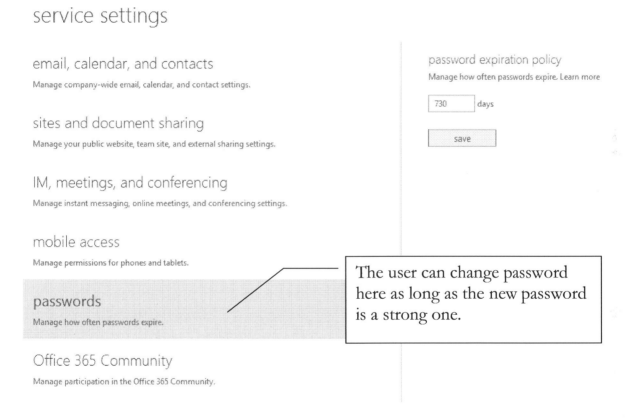

Facebook contact synchronization is a feature for connecting between a Facebook account and an Office 365 account via OWA. With it, Facebook friends will be listed as contacts in Office 365 as well. This feature is on by default (not all regions support this feature though). LinkedIn contact synchronization is similar, just that it involves LinkedIn contacts.

Facebook contact sync

Let people add Facebook friends as contacts in their address book.
Learn more

ON

LinkedIn contact sync

Let people add LinkedIn connections as contacts in their address
book. Learn more

ON

In any case, to start a connection to these accounts, from within OWA you go to Settings - Options - Account - Connected accounts and check out the Connect Office 365 to your networks section. OR, from People you click Connect to social network.

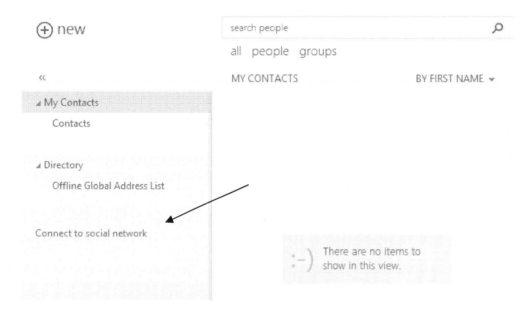

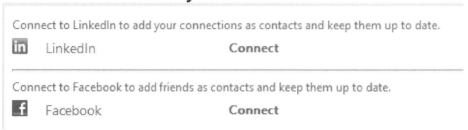

connect Office 365 to your networks

Connect to LinkedIn to add your connections as contacts and keep them up to date.

|in| LinkedIn   **Connect**

Connect to Facebook to add friends as contacts and keep them up to date.

|f| Facebook   **Connect**

service settings

email, calendar, and contacts

Manage company-wide email, calendar, and contact settings.

sites and document sharing

Manage your public website, team site, and external sharing settings.

IM, meetings, and conferencing

Manage instant messaging, online meetings, and conferencing settings.

mobile access

Manage permissions for phones and tablets.

passwords

Manage how often passwords expire.

Office 365 Community ⟵

Manage participation in the Office 365 Community.

Office 365 Community participat

Let people participate in the Office 365 Commi
365 user ID. Learn more

ON

When participation is turned on, users who browse the Office 365 community can post questions and comments to the forums using either an Office 365 user ID or a MS account. Do note that after you turn on community participation, it may take 24 hours for the change to become effective. If you turn it off, community content posted will not be affected in any way.

User and group management

You use users & groups to add new users.

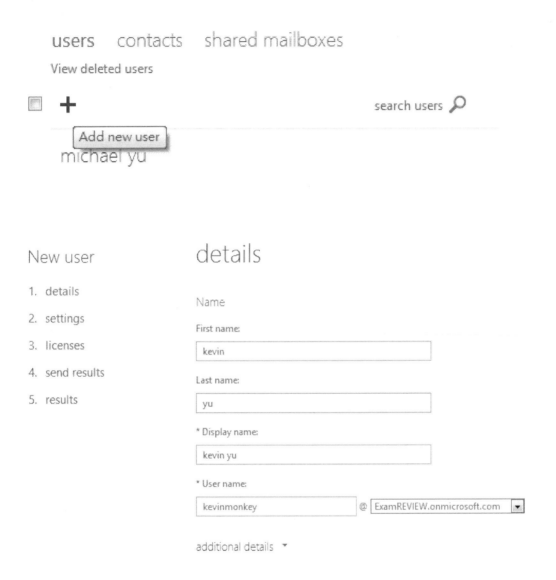

users & groups

users   contacts   shared mailboxes

View deleted users

☐ +

Add new user

michael yu

search users 🔍

New user

1. details
2. settings
3. licenses
4. send results
5. results

details

Name

First name:

kevin

Last name:

yu

* Display name:

kevin yu

* User name:

kevinmonkey   @   ExamREVIEW.onmicrosoft.com ▼

additional details ▼

When you add a new user, you can choose to give this new user the permissions necessary for performing the various admin tasks.

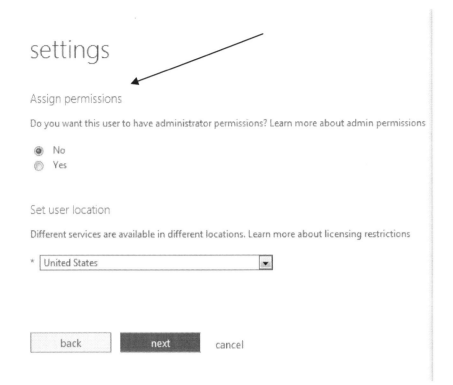

settings

Assign permissions

Do you want this user to have administrator permissions? Learn more about admin permissions

○ No
○ Yes

Set user location

Different services are available in different locations. Learn more about licensing restrictions

* [United States ▼]

[back] [next] cancel

In terms of groups, note that under the Site settings of SharePoint online there are 4 groups by default, which are members, visitors, owners and Excel Services viewers.

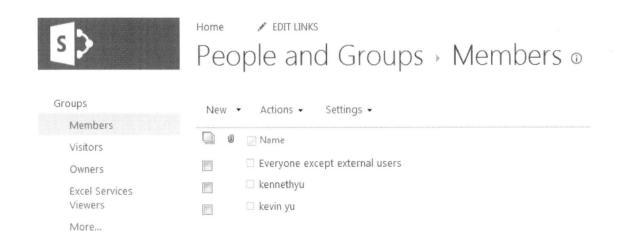

Home   ✎ EDIT LINKS

People and Groups ⟩ Members ⓘ

Groups

Members

Visitors

Owners

Excel Services
Viewers

More...

New ▾   Actions ▾   Settings ▾

☐ ⦿ ☐ Name
☐   ☐ Everyone except external users
☐   ☐ kennethyu
☐   ☐ kevin yu

You may add or remove users from these groups. However, the interface does not allow you to create new groups here (you need to do this somewhere else).

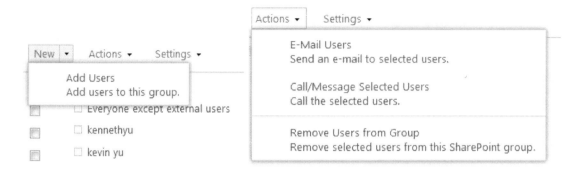

Other groups that are available if you click More include Company Administrator (it covers all Office 365 admins, including the Global and Billing admins), Everyone (this definition includes also the external users), and Everyone except External Users (it excludes those you add explicitly as external users). You can click Edit to further edit group membership and properties such as group name, owner, description ..etc.

Do note that Site Collection Administrators is a group with full control over all SharePoint sites in the site collection. By default all company admins belong to this group.

Site Collection Administrators

Site Collection
Administrators
Site Collection
Administrators are given full
control over all Web sites in
the site collection. They may
also receive site use
confirmation mail. Enter
users separated by
semicolons.

Company Administrator x

ExamREVIEW Team Site › People and Groups ⓘ

New ▾   Settings ▾

Group	Edit	About me
Company Administrator	🖉	
Everyone	🖉	
Everyone except external users	🖉	
Excel Services Viewers	🖉	Members of this group can view pages, list items, and documents. If the document has a s using the server rendering.
Members	🖉	Use this group to grant people contribute permissions to the SharePoint site:
Owners	🖉	Use this group to grant people full control permissions to the SharePoint site:
Visitors	🖉	Use this group to grant people read permissions to the SharePoint site:

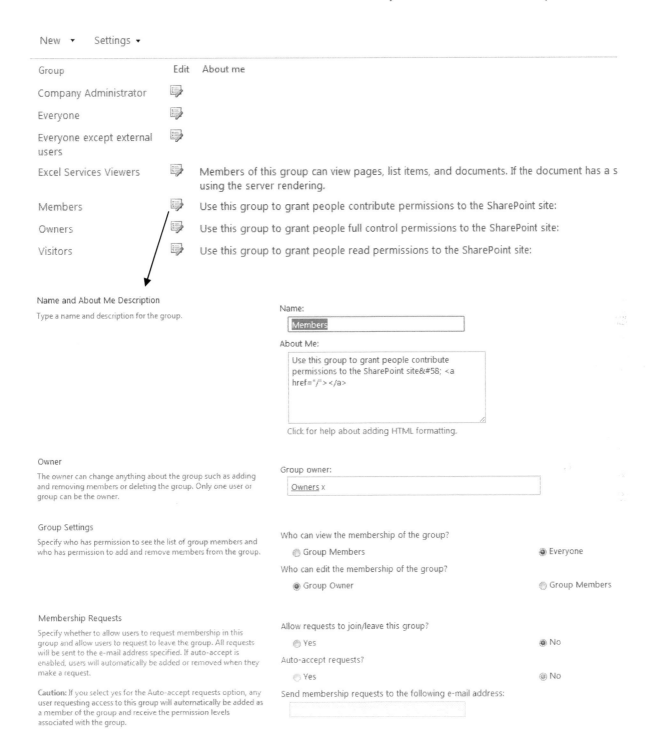

Name and About Me Description

Type a name and description for the group.

Name:

Members

About Me:

Use this group to grant people contribute permissions to the SharePoint site: <a href="/"></a>

Click for help about adding HTML formatting.

Owner

The owner can change anything about the group such as adding and removing members or deleting the group. Only one user or group can be the owner.

Group owner:

Owners x

Group Settings

Specify who has permission to see the list of group members and who has permission to add and remove members from the group.

Who can view the membership of the group?

◯ Group Members   ◉ Everyone

Who can edit the membership of the group?

◉ Group Owner   ◯ Group Members

Membership Requests

Specify whether to allow users to request membership in this group and allow users to request to leave the group. All requests will be sent to the e-mail address specified. If auto-accept is enabled, users will automatically be added or removed when they make a request.

Caution: If you select yes for the Auto-accept requests option, any user requesting access to this group will automatically be added as a member of the group and receive the permission levels associated with the group.

Allow requests to join/leave this group?

◯ Yes   ◉ No

Auto-accept requests?

◯ Yes   ◉ No

Send membership requests to the following e-mail address:

Admin roles

To be precise, Office 365 has several different types of administrator roles as defined by MS, including Billing admin (available in Office 365 for enterprises only since billing changes cannot be made in other offerings), global admin (which is you if you are the one who signed up and bought Office 365), password admin, service admin, and user management admin. Full administration possesses privileges equivalent to those of global administrator. Limited administration possesses privileges equivalent to those of password administrator.

MS refers to the use of roles as RBAC. Roles can be thought of as collections of permissions to use resources appropriate to a staff's job function. This works with the assumption that all permissions needed to perform a job function can be neatly encapsulated.

The thing is, this role based model is not available in the Small Business offering. In the Small Business offering, an user is either an admin or not an admin – no roles can be assigned.

Bulk importing users

Bulk importing users is not possible via the portal as of the time of this writing. You need to prepare a CSV file and use the Powershell to do the job. First you need to make sure PowerShell is working fine with Office 365. Then you use a text editor to prepare a .csv file (say, newusers.csv) with the attributes of user principal name, display name, last name, first name and other information included. Then you connect to Windows Azure with PowerShell, and run:

Import-Csv .\newusers.csv | foreach{New-MsolUser -UserPrincipalName $_.Name -DisplayName $_.Display -FirstName $_.First -LastName $_.Last}

The details of setting up Powershell are separately discussed. Keep in mind, to avoid code issue you should save the CSV file in a Unicode or UTF-8 format. The first row always contains only user data column labels. The max number of rows allowed in the file is 251 including the first row. You should use a separate CSV file for each region and perform bulk import separately. *Office 365 for enterprises does have a Bulk Add Users wizard and a CSV template available.*

Do note that bulk importing contacts (via CSV file) is different. You can do it from the portal:

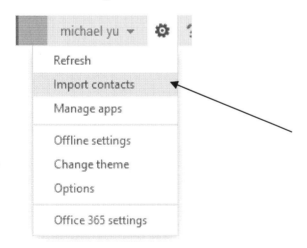

Assigning licenses and resetting passwords

In fact, as the first administrator you must assign a license to yourself so you can configure features such as public web site:

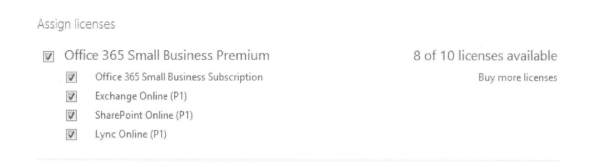

Assigning license is a necessary step if you want a new user to be able to actually use Office 365. When you create a new user account, a license should be associated with the user so he can access the Office 365 services. Keep in mind, only the admin user can edit user accounts and change license assignment. According to MS, Small Business subscribers will receive only Windows Azure Active Directory cloud credentials for signing in.

Also note that not all services are available in all locations, and that a conflict will occur if you do not have enough licenses for your users. When there is a conflict, you may choose to either remove a license from an existing user or delete a user account altogether to free a license. In fact, when you bulk edit a group of users, there are options for you to change or reassign licenses.

assign licenses

- ⦿ Retain current license assignments
- ○ Replace existing license assignments
- ○ Add to existing license assignments

☐ Office 365 Small Business Premium   8 of 10 licenses available
   ☐ Office 365 Small Business Subscription
   ☐ Exchange Online (P1)
   ☐ SharePoint Online (P1)
   ☐ Lync Online (P1)

You may also go to the License section and click Purchase Services to purchase licenses:

licenses

subscriptions   **purchase services**

Office 365 plans | Other plans

Office 365 plans ▲

Office 365 Small Business Premium Trial

For small businesses and professionals (less than 25 users) that need Office suite, email, instant messaging, document/content management, web conferencing. Includes Microsoft Office for Windows, Mac, mobile and Office Web Apps. Simple setup and deployment.

Currently in trial   Buy now

Office 365 Small Business

For small businesses (fewer than 25 users) and professionals that need anywhere access to email and documents with Office Web Apps. $60.00
per user license, per year

Learn more   Add 🛒

You may allow confirmation email to be sent to you, detailing the result of user creation. And very importantly, there is a temporary password for first time login and the link to the login page!

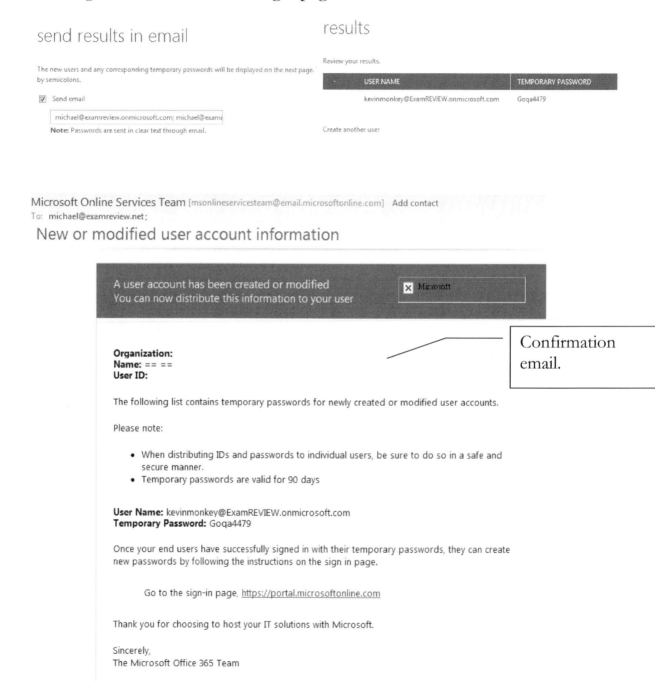

send results in email

The new users and any corresponding temporary passwords will be displayed on the next page. by semicolons.

☑ Send email

michael@examreview.onmicrosoft.com; michael@exami

Note: Passwords are sent in clear text through email.

results

Review your results.

USER NAME	TEMPORARY PASSWORD
kevinmonkey@ExamREVIEW.onmicrosoft.com	Goqa4479

Create another user

Microsoft Online Services Team [msonlineservicesteam@email.microsoftonline.com]   Add contact
To: michael@examreview.net;

New or modified user account information

A user account has been created or modified
You can now distribute this information to your user   ☒ Microsoft

Organization:
Name: == ==
User ID:

Confirmation email.

The following list contains temporary passwords for newly created or modified user accounts.

Please note:

- When distributing IDs and passwords to individual users, be sure to do so in a safe and secure manner.
- Temporary passwords are valid for 90 days

User Name: kevinmonkey@ExamREVIEW.onmicrosoft.com
Temporary Password: Goqa4479

Once your end users have successfully signed in with their temporary passwords, they can create new passwords by following the instructions on the sign in page.

Go to the sign-in page, https://portal.microsoftonline.com

Thank you for choosing to host your IT solutions with Microsoft.

Sincerely,
The Microsoft Office 365 Team

User Name: kevinmonkey@ExamREVIEW.onmicrosoft.com
Temporary Password: (xxxx44/79)

Once your end users have successfully signed in with their temporary pas
new passwords by following the instructions on the sign in page.

Go to the sign-in page, https://portal.microsoftonline.com

Every new user will be assigned an unchangeable unique identifier which looks like this: 1003BFFD870CC5EA. When his first logins, he will be asked to set a new password, which must be a strong password with at least 8 characters but no more than 16 (this password should have lowercase and uppercase characters plus numbers or symbols).

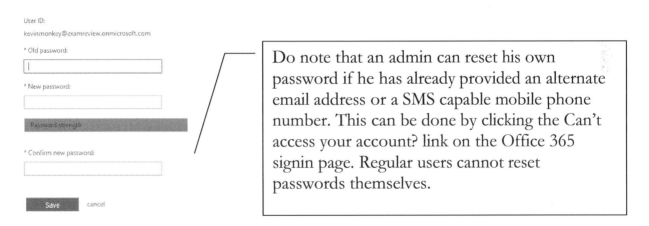

Do note that an admin can reset his own password if he has already provided an alternate email address or a SMS capable mobile phone number. This can be done by clicking the Can't access your account? link on the Office 365 signin page. Regular users cannot reset passwords themselves.

This new user will have his own Office 365 settings section, allowing him to install software and perform other basic settings on password and contacts.

Office 365 settings

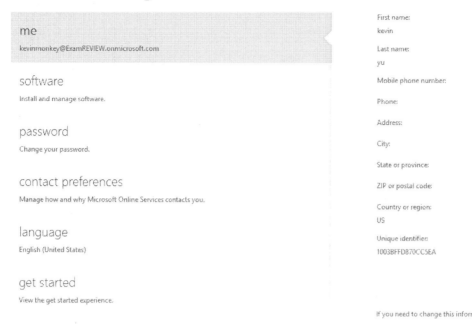

me
kevinmonkey@ExamREVIEW.onmicrosoft.com

software
Install and manage software.

password
Change your password.

contact preferences
Manage how and why Microsoft Online Services contacts you.

language
English (United States)

get started
View the get started experience.

First name:
kevin

Last name:
yu

Mobile phone number:

Phone:

Address:

City:

State or province:

ZIP or postal code:

Country or region:
US

Unique identifier:
1003BFFD870CC5EA

If you need to change this inforr

If the user chooses to edit the About Me page, he can edit his profile and even upload a profile picture.

If you need to change this information, contact your admin.

Add information about me to share with my coworkers.
Edit my About me page ⓘ

kevin yu

About me
People

About kevin yu

⊘ edit your profile
Tell others about yourself and share your areas of expertise by editing your profile.

We're almost ready!

While we set things up, feel free to change your photo, adjust your personal settings, and fill in information about yourself.

It could take us a while, but once we're done, here's what you'll get:

Newsfeed is your social hub where you'll see updates from the people, documents, sites, and tags you're following, with quick access to the apps you've added.

SkyDrive Pro is your personal hard drive in the cloud, the place you can store, share, and sync your work files.

Sites gives you easy access to the places you'll want to go.

Edit Details

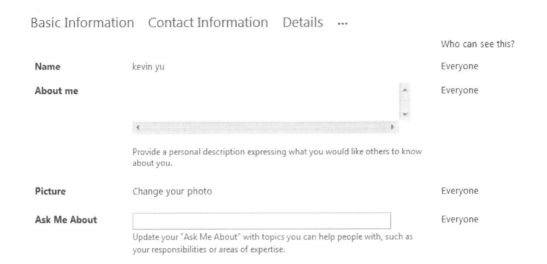

Basic Information   Contact Information   Details   ...

		Who can see this?
Name	kevin yu	Everyone
About me		Everyone
	Provide a personal description expressing what you would like others to know about you.	
Picture	Change your photo	Everyone
Ask Me About		Everyone
	Update your "Ask Me About" with topics you can help people with, such as your responsibilities or areas of expertise.	

The details can be viewable by only the user himself or every coworker.

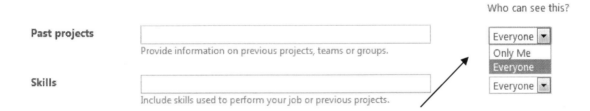

		Who can see this?
Past projects		Everyone ▾
	Provide information on previous projects, teams or groups.	Only Me / Everyone
Skills		Everyone ▾
	Include skills used to perform your job or previous projects.	

You as the admin can also change their settings. You can select multiple users and perform a bulk edit:

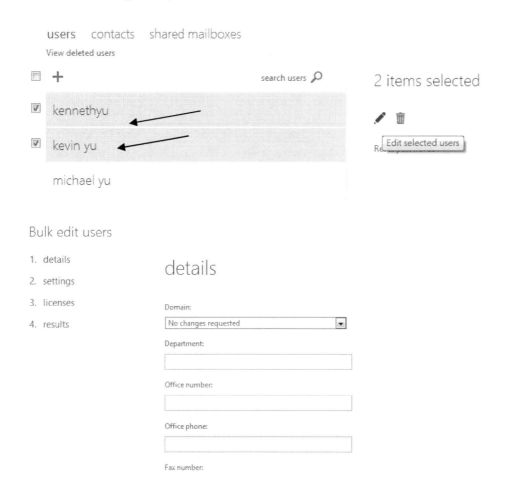

users & groups

users   contacts   shared mailboxes

View deleted users

+   search users 🔍

☑ kennethyu

☑ kevin yu

   michael yu

2 items selected

✏ 🗑

Edit selected users

Bulk edit users

1. details
2. settings
3. licenses
4. results

details

Domain:

No changes requested ▾

Department:

Office number:

Office phone:

Fax number:

In fact, editing permissions, sign-in status (allowed or blocked) and location via bulk edit can be very convenient:

Bulk edit users

1. details
2. settings
3. licenses
4. results

settings

Assign permissions

Do you want the users you selected to have administrator permissions? Learn more about admi

- ◉ No changes requested
- ○ No
- ○ Yes

Set sign-in status

- ◉ No changes requested
- ○ Allowed
  Users can sign in and access services.
- ○ Blocked
  Users can't sign in or access services.

Set user location

Different services are available in different locations. Learn more about licensing restrictions

| No changes requested | ▾ |

Shared mailboxes and contacts

A common shared mailbox can be used by multiple users to send and receive emails. You can add multiple users to it. According to MS, a common mailbox is a great way for handling customer queries.

common

Shared mailboxes make it easy for more than one user to monitor an

* Mailbox name:

| common |

This name will appear in the shared address book and the To: line in email.

* Email address:

| commonbox | @ ExamREVIEW.onmicrosoft.com

Example: info@contoso.com

Members

➕

kennethyu ⬅

kevin yu ⬅

From the user end, access to this mailbox can be done through Outlook (OWA or Outlook desktop client) once signed in to Outlook. In the context of Outlook, a shared mailbox is in a sense a form of Delegate Access.

External contacts represent those email recipients who are NOT inside your organization (they have e-mail addresses that do not belong to your domain nor your organization - they just don't have a mailbox in your environment). These contacts can be added as a shared contact.

add a shared contact

Add people from outside your organization to the shared address book so everyone can use them. Learn more

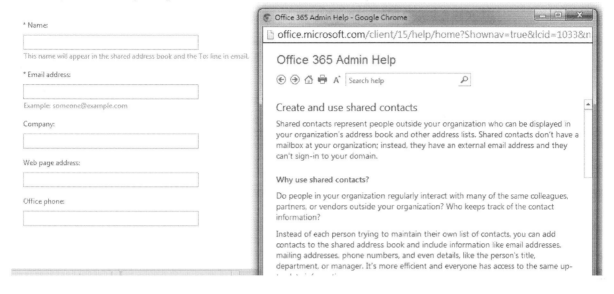

* Name:

This name will appear in the shared address book and the To: line in email.

* Email address:

Example: someone@example.com

Company:

Web page address:

Office phone:

add a shared contact

Add people from outside your organization to the share

* Name:

kenneth

This name will appear in the shared address book and the To: line in email.

* Email address:

kenneth@monkey.com

Example: someone@example.com

Company:

monkeyschool

Office Pro Plus

Through the software section the user can install MS Office Pro Plus onto the local client computer. In 2013 there is a service upgrade bringing in new features. With the Office 365 Small Business Premium offering, each user can install the latest version of Office on max 5 computers (compatible with PCs or Macs).

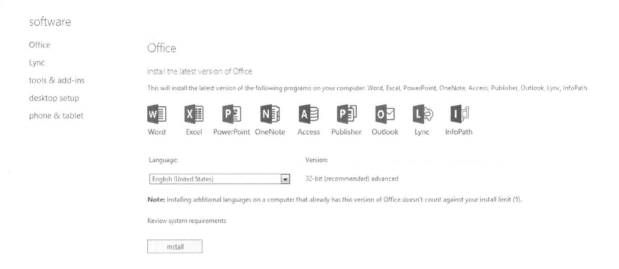

The local system must be running Windows Server 2008 R2, Windows 7/8 or Windows Server 2012, with at least 1GB RAM and 3GB drive space. The processor needs to support SSE2 instruction set. .NET framework 3.5 or later must be available.

Office Pro Plus are available in 32 bit and 64 bit formats. You can click Advanced to choose the version you want to install. You can also choose a language version. The default is 32 bit, which can run fine on 32bit/64bit

Windows (Windows 7/Windows 8 only - XP and Vista cannot run Office Pro Plus).

If the 5-computer limitation is reached, it is possible to deactivate an installation so to free up a quota. All you need to do is to go to Software -> Office and click Deactivate on the desired computer.

Technet evaluation center also allows trial download to be retrieved. According to Technet, since Office Pro Plus will run in a sandbox, it will not affect your existing Office software. The trial can allow max 25 evaluators within an organization:

MS has a Fix-It software you can use to troubleshoot problems encountered. It can be found here: http://support.microsoft.com/kb/2822317/en-us

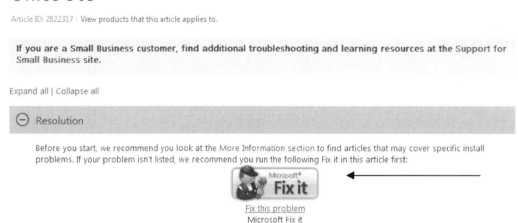

General troubleshooting for installing Office 2013 and Office 365

Article ID: 2822317 - View products that this article applies to.

If you are a Small Business customer, find additional troubleshooting and learning resources at the Support for Small Business site.

Expand all | Collapse all

⊖ Resolution

Before you start, we recommend you look at the More Information section to find articles that may cover specific install problems. If your problem isn't listed, we recommend you run the following Fix it in this article first:

Microsoft® **Fix it**

Fix this problem
Microsoft Fix it

Domains

As previously mentioned, Office 365 Small Business will create a domain for you at the time you sign up. You CANNOT delete this domain.

ExamREVIEW.onmicrosoft.com

DNS management
Initial domain: This domain is included with your account. It's set up automatically for you, and you can't delete it.

domain status
Active

Return to Domains list

If you have your own domain, you can click Add a domain to add it to Office 365.

domains

Your Office 365 account comes with a domain name—*contoso*.onmicrosoft.com—but if you have your own domain name already, you can use that dom
services too. To add your domain, click **Add a domain**.

If you don't already own a domain name, you can purchase one from a domain registrar, and then come back to add it to Office 365.

Add a domain | Remove | Manage DNS | Troubleshoot

	Domain name ▲	Status
○	ExamREVIEW.onmicrosoft.com	Active

Add a domain | Remove | Manage DNS | Troubleshoot

You can have one domain active for your email addresses. Therefore, if you add a domain, your existing email address's domain part will be changed. Any web site address will also be changed.

Change your Office 365 email address to use *@yourcompany.com*

Why change it?

When you signed up, your initial Office 365 email address was **michael@examreview.onmicrosoft.com**.

But if you already own an email address that your customers are familiar with, like **michael@yourcompany.com**, you can use that address instead. Do I have to do this be

Get an overview of the process:
Video: Customize your email address in Office 365

Would you like to change your Office 365 email address now?

It will take about **45 minutes** to make the change, and we'll show you exactly what to do. Why will it take so long?

Start now   Maybe later

In fact, this dialog can also be reached through the email address section.

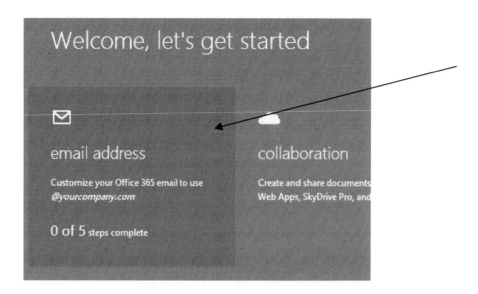

You need to understand how DNS works. DNS Domain Name System is for name resolution. It performs name-to-IP mapping per the request of the client devices. A DNS name has at least two parts separated by periods. The rightmost is the top-level domain while the other parts are subdomains, which usually refer to the owner organization.

In a traditional setup with your own Exchange Server hosted in- house, the DNS MX record must link your Exchange server to the email domain name. Your ISP may have a MX record for your domain pointing to the ISP's name servers, therefore you must regularly download emails from the ISP's mail server to your own Exchange server. OR you may have a permanent IP address which is always connected to the internet such that the MX records on your own DNS would point to your own Exchange servers. Any email addressed to the external recipients must be processed with the help of a DNS server with root hints, which possess IP addresses of those internet servers that which specialize in top level domains. Either your own DNS server should have root hints configured, or that you forward all external emails to the ISP's DNS server.

With Office 365, Exchange Online needs to take over. Therefore DNS will be modified to point to Exchange Online so that emails can be retrieved from there. Exchange Online requires a MX record for email routing, a CNAME record that help users to set up a connection via autodiscovery, and a TXT/SPF record which allows outlook.com to send email on behalf of your own domain.

Lync Online also requires some DNS records. It needs some SRV records to support instant messaging, presence, and meeting sign-in. It also needs CNAME records for autodiscovery by desktop and mobile clients.

Before you add your own domain, make sure you already own it.

Add a domain

If you own a domain already, you can have Office 365 email a a website address like *www.yourcompany.com*.

What domain do you want to use with Office 365? What's a domain?

examreview.net

Example: fourthcoffee.com

MS must verify domain ownership first before going ahead.

confirm that you own examreview.net

Before you set up your domain with Office 365, we have to make sure that you own the domain name. T for the record to confirm ownership.

Note: This doesn't affect how your domain works. Learn more

See step-by-step instructions for performing this step with: (DNS hosting provider) ▼

Note that if you already have a web site hosted somewhere else using this domain name, MS cannot migrate it to Office 365 for you.

Change your Office 365 email address to use @examreview.net

Tell us about **examreview.net**

Do people in your company already have **examreview.net** email addresses?

- ○ Yes
- ○ No

Do you already have a **examreview.net** website? Why is this important?

- ○ Yes, and I want to keep it where it's hosted today
- ○ Yes, but I want to design a new website in Office 365 to replace it
- ○ No

Note: Unfortunately, we can't automatically move your website from your current website host to Office 365.

When you add your domain to Office 365, you may need to update the corresponding name server records to point to the Office 365-hosted name servers so to allow Office 365 to manage these records. This is the recommended approach if you want to simplify the setup process. However, if you want to manage DNS using your own DNS solution, then you must configure the required DNS records yourself. To be precise, you need to change DNS records for Exchange Online and Lync Online on your DNS platform. *Do note that DNS of the domain created by Office 365 cannot be managed by you.*

Sending and retrieving emails

You may use Outlook Web App OWA to access your Office 365 email account. A wide variety of browsers can work, and you should check the latest list via this link:

http://office.microsoft.com/en-001/web-apps-help/supported-browsers-for-outlook-web-app-HA102824601.aspx?CTT=5&origin=HA102821290

In fact, when you login to your Office 365 account, you can access OWA – no separate installation is necessary. You can use it to send emails as usual.

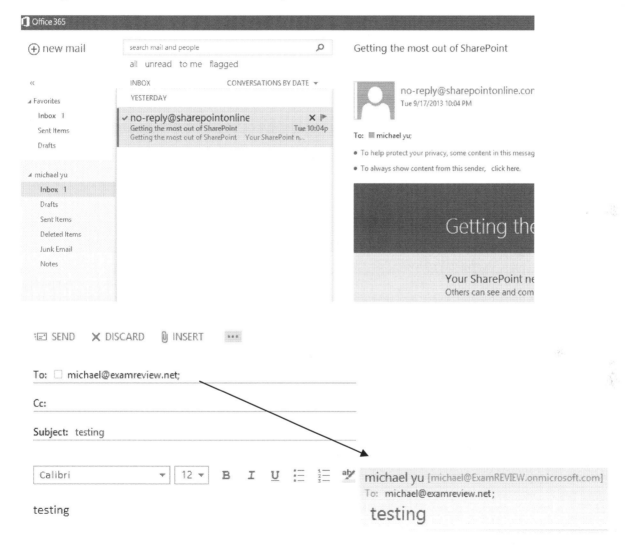

The Calendar function can also be used for scheduling just like the desktop version:

And you may sign in to Instant Messaging IM and present a status:

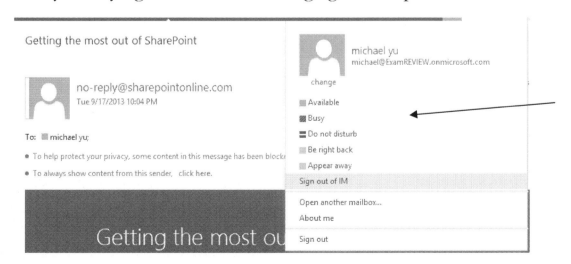

You may also use the Outlook desktop client. Office 365 supports Outlook 2007, 2010 and 2013. However, they may not be installed on the same computer simultaneously. From within Outlook you need to add account, then from within the Add New Account dialog box you select Email Account and enter your name (as well as email address and password) necessary for accessing your Office 365 account. Outlook will connect to Exchange for Office 365 and automatically configures Outlook accordingly.

Web presence

The Public Website is in fact a part of SharePoint Online, which can be customized as much as possible. You can manage the site address or design your public web site.

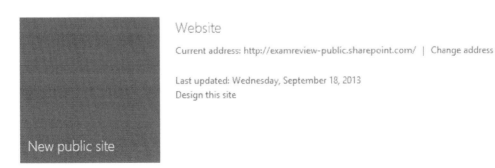

Manage public website

Before you can change your public website address to something that's easier to remember, like www.fourthcoffee.com, you have to first add the address to Office 365.

Website

Current address: http://examreview-public.sharepoint.com/ | Change address

Last updated: Wednesday, September 18, 2013
Design this site

New public site

You can stick with the default domain URL provided by MS, or pick a domain you have added. The default address is your account name followed by –public and then by .sharepoint.com.

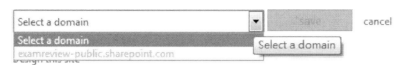

Website

Select a domain	▼
Select a domain	
examreview-public.sharepoint.com	

Save   cancel

Select a domain

When you click Design this site, Office 365 will get you into a web design tool for arranging and designing web pages:

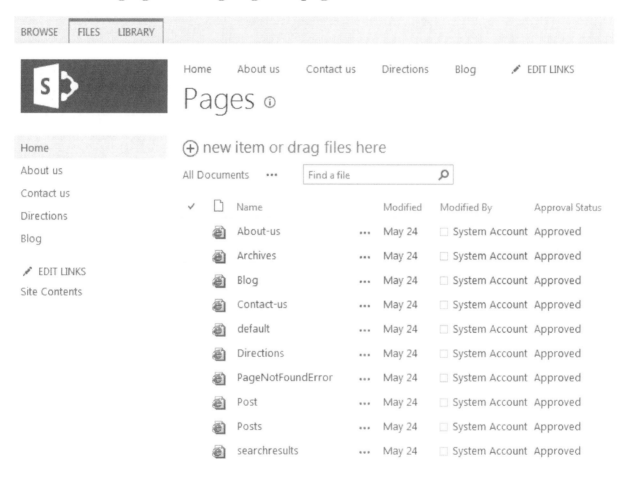

From within the Site Settings page you may access features such as site collection settings, web design galleries and Design Manager.

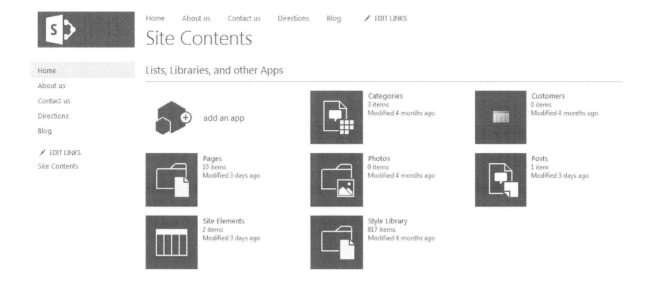

The permissions you have determine your level of access to the website and the Site Design Tool. If you have Full Control (or Designer permission), you can have full access to all the available tools. Some customizations apply to the whole site, while others apply to some pages only. Site customizations are global level changes you make to affect all pages. They include:

- site theme and style

- site navigation

- site color schemes and fonts

- header and footer text to every page

Page customizations, on the other hand, apply to individual pages. They include:

- Adding, editing and formatting text

- Adding and editing page elements

- Adding gadgets, which are standalone applications that aim to make the web pages more dynamic.

Workflows

Workflow is in fact a feature of SharePoint – they are pre-programmed for automating business processes. Do note that SharePoint Online can only support sandboxed solutions, that all code-based workflows are not allowed to run at all.

Home   About us   Contact us   Directions   Blog   ✏ EDIT LINKS

Workflows: Website ⓘ

Start a New Workflow

This site has no workflows to start.

Workflows

Select a workflow to view more details.   Show all workflows.

Name	Started	Ended
My Running Workflows		

There are no running workflows on this site.

My Completed Workflows

There are no completed workflows on this site.

From the tools & add-in section you can download the SharePoint Designer, which can be used to design workflows (and SharePoint sites).

tools & add-ins

SharePoint Designer 2013

Use SharePoint Designer 2013 to create workflows and modify the look and feel of your SharePoint sites.

Language: Version:

| English (United States)   ▼ |

32-bit (recommended) advanced

Service status

Current status is for tracking service health (service availability as well as service disruption and outage). You want to know the types of status available.

current status   planned maintenance

Last refreshed: 7:35 PM, September 17, 2013

SERVICE	TODAY	SEP 16
Exchange Online ▼	✓	✓
Identity Service ▼	✓	✓
Lync Online ▲		
All Features	✓	✓
Audio and Video	✓	✓
Dial-In Conferencing	✓	✓
Federation	✓	✓
Instant Messaging	✓	✓
Management and Provisioning	✓	✓
Mobility	✓	✓
Online Meetings	✓	✓
Presence	✓	✓
Sign-In	✓	✓

| ✔ Normal service | ⑦ Investigating | ⬇ Service interruption |
| 🔄 Extended recovery | ✅ Service restored | ⓘ Additional information |

Learn more about service health status

| ➡ Service degradation | ↻ Restoring service |
| ☐ PIR published | |

Normal means the service is available and is running normally as usual. Investigating means there is a potential service incident currently under investigation. False positive means the service is actually healthy. Service interruption means the service is not functioning at all. Restoring service means the service problem is being resolved.

Service degradation means the service is still there but is in a poor condition. Extended recovery means it is going to take some time for the service to be normal again. Normal service restored means things are fine now. Post-incident report published means there is a report published concerning the incident. Timing is based on the time of YOUR location.

SkyDrive Pro

SkyDrive Pro is a cloud based storage drive. You can keep your stuff private until you share them. It is supposed to serve as a replacement for My Documents. By default SkyDrive Pro offers a 25GB storage with a max upload size of 2GB (http://sharepointpromag.com/office-365/updates-sharepoint-online-september-5-2013):

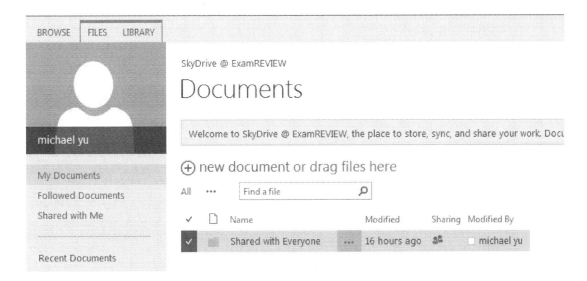

The same interface can be used to check if someone else is sharing things with you.

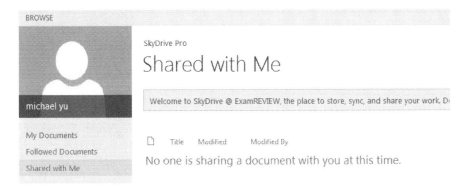

Synchronizing directories

You may want to synchronize your own directory with the one running in the cloud. When you synchronize the directories, a copy of your local users and groups will be to the Windows Azure AD. AD will then track checks and make updates accordingly. With the Windows Azure Active Directory Sync tool Configuration Wizard, a MSOL_AD_SYNC account will be created in your local forest. This is a service account that will be used to synchronize directory information. By default recurring synchronizations will take place every 3 hours. If this MSOL_AD_SYNC account is corrupted, synchronization will fail. Also, by default you can't synchronize more than 50000 directory objects.

Keep in mind, the computer performing directory synchronization must run Windows Server 2008 R2 or later (it must be a server OS), and must be joined to AD. However, it cannot be a domain controller. .NET Framework 3.5 SP1 or later must be installed, and Windows PowerShell must be enabled.

When the synchronization process creates mail-enabled users in Office 365, the same user principal name UPN will be used. However, passwords will NOT be synchronized by default. We refer to the "new" accounts created in the cloud as a result of synchronization as managed identities. Users must use two sets of passwords - one for the local environment and another for Office 365. With SSO, through identity federation only the original local credentials are required. It is recommended that the AD FS be properly configured in your local environment before configuring the directory synchronization tools.

Setting up Powershell

The Windows Azure Active Directory Module for PowerShell needs to be downloaded in order to manage data in Windows Azure AD via Powershell (Windows PowerShell 2.0 or later). There are 2 versions, which are 32-bit and 64-bit. From this link you can download the necessary msi file:

http://technet.microsoft.com/library/jj151815.aspx

Install the Windows Azure AD Module

You must install the appropriate version of the Windows Azure AD Module for Windows PowerShell for your operating sy

- Windows Azure Active Directory Module for Windows PowerShell (32-bit version)

- Windows Azure Active Directory Module for Windows PowerShell (64-bit version)

◆ **Important**

If you are using Windows PowerShell 2.0 and Single Sign-On, you must use at least Windows PowerShell 2.0, and you mu
so, you can use Windows PowerShell remoting. For information, see About_Remote_Requirements.

When properly configured, there will be a Windows Azure Active Directory Module for Windows PowerShell shortcut you can use to invoke it. You may also load the cmdlets via import-module MSOnline at the PowerShell prompt. To connect to the online service, run connect-msolservice. To seek help on a cmdlet, use get-help <cmdlet-name> -detailed.

The essential PowerShell commands

Each time you start Windows PowerShell you are only in the session of your local computer, which is a client-side session. You need to connect to the cloud in order to open up a server-side session. You use $LiveCred = Get-Credential and then type in the credentials of your cloud account, then use $Session = New-PSSession to open a session specific to the application you use. You then use Import-PSSession $Session to import the necessary commands to your client-side session. And you may later use Remove-PSSession to disconnect from the server-side session.

For exam prep purpose you need to remember these commands:

Commands dealing with user objects

You use Get-MsolUser to retrieve either an individual user or a list of users. You use Set-MsolUser to update a user object. You use New-MsolUser to create a new user, or use Remove-MsolUser to remove one. You may optionally use Restore-MsolUser to restore a deleted user (if the user is still in the Deleted users view). You use Set-MsolUserPassword to change the user password, or use Set-MsolUserPrincipalName to edit the User Principal Name.

Commands dealing with user groups

You use Add-MsolGroupMember to add members to a group, or use Get-MsolGroup to retrieve a group. Get-MsolGroupMember can be used to retrieve members of a specific group. New-MsolGroup can be used to create a new group. Remove-MsolGroup is for deleting a group, while Remove-MsolGroupMember cmdlet is for removing a member from a group. You may also use Set-MsolGroup to update the group properties.

Commands dealing with user roles

You use Add-MsolRoleMember to add a user (not a group) to a role. You use Get-MsolRole to retrieve a list of admin roles, or use Get-MsolUserRole to retrieve all the admin roles that a specified user is belonging to. Get-MsolRoleMember can be used to retrieve all members of a specific role. Remove-MsolRoleMember can be used to remove a user from an admin role.

Commands for managing subscriptions, licenses, partners contacts and director synchronization

You use Get-MsolSubscription to find out about all the subscriptions you have purchased. Get-MsolAccountSku shows all the SKUs you own. New-MsolLicenseOptions is for creating a new License Options object, while Set-MsolUserLicense is for adjusting the user licenses.

You use Set-MsolDirSyncEnabled to switch on or off directory synchronization. You use Get-MsolPartnerInformation to retrieve partner-specific information, or use Set-MsolPartnerInformation to configure partner-specific properties. You use Get-MsolContact to retrieve a contact, or use Remove-MsolContact to delete one.

Exchange Online Email Migration and other mail settings

You may use E-Mail Migration from within the Exchange Control Panel if you want to migrate emails to the cloud. Assuming that your Exchange organization is an accepted domain of your cloud-based organization (this is a MUST), you may migrate mailboxes and mailbox data from Exchange Server 2013, 2010, 2007, and even 2003. You may also migrate mailbox data only from an IMAP system. With a cutover migration, all on-premises mailboxes will be migrated with the goal of moving the whole email organization to Office 365. However, there is a limit - according to MS you can migrate max 1000 mailboxes this way. Also, you will need to assign licenses accordingly.

If you are migrating from Exchange 2007 or later, Autodiscover can automatically detect the connection settings. With Exchange 2003, you must specify the connection settings by hand. Note that when performing the migration, the address book from your original Exchange server will be used to identify the mailboxes, distribution groups, and contacts to migrate. In fact, the actual migration process involves provisioning new cloud-based mailboxes and recreating the distribution groups and contacts. There will be an initial synchronization process followed by incremental synchronization which takes place every 24 hours.

A CSV file may be used for migration. Every such file can have max 50000 rows with one row per user. The file cannot be larger than 10 MB in size. You may use multiple files and perform migration one after another. Inside the file you must provide the username and password for the user's local account. You may obtain their passwords or change their passwords to a value that you are aware of and then perform the migration, or you may use an admin account which gives you access to everything. Regarding the file syntax, this file must use comma separated formatting and must include the required attributes in the header row (which is the first row). It must contain the Password attribute plus attributes that can be recognized by the import process. Very importantly, the user rows must have the same number of attributes as the header.

When migrating Exchange users you should require them to change their password via the ForceChangePassword attribute (this is for the sake of security). The DisplayName attribute is optional. Should you want to use both the LastName and the FirstName as the format for the display name, when preparing the CSV file you use double quotes in the DisplayName attribute value.

If you want to maintain mailboxes both locally and in the cloud, you should deploy Exchange via hybrid deployment. For this to work, you need to run Exchange Server 2010 or later. You do not need to have a full scale installation though - even a minimal Exchange hybrid server will work. To be precise, the hybrid server must run Exchange 2010 SP3 or Exchange 2013 CU2. It is a bridge between the local Exchange environment and Exchange Online. Keep in mind, there is no need to upgrade the existing local Exchange mailboxes to Exchange 2010 or Exchange 2013 for a hybrid deployment to work. The Windows Azure Active Directory Sync tool must be running in your local environment. The Microsoft Federation Gateway as a free online service (one that acts as a trust broker) must also be used - a federation trust needs to be created with the Microsoft Federation Gateway.

Room mailboxes are special resource based mailboxes - you use them to reserve physical "rooms" by sending to these mailboxes meeting requests. Delegates are held responsible for either accepting or declining meeting requests. There is no way users can sign in to a room's mailbox, but it has a calendar shared by default so users can access it via OWA. Equipment mailboxes are similar - they do not have physical locations but are representing real world equipments.

Distribution groups are collections of recipients that appear in the shared address book. When an email message reaches a group, it simply goes to all members of the group. A distribution group can be organized by a particular discussion subject or by users sharing a common work structure. You may view or change the properties of a group via the Exchange Control Panel or the Office 365 portal.

distribution groups

A distribution group is a collection of two or more people in an organization's shared address book. You can create groups, which will appear in the address book for others t can also join or leave an existing group.

distribution groups I belong to

type the name of the group you're looking for

Display name	Email address

There are no items to show in this view.

distribution groups I own

type the name of the group you're looking for

Display name	Email ad

:¨¨: Pleas

When you use OWA to manage mail settings, there are a bunch of options to play with.

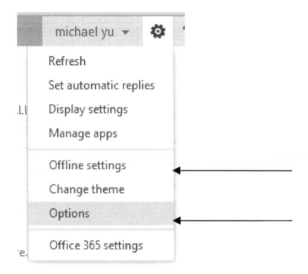

With offline settings, you can allow offline access (which is in fact a form of caching).

✓ OK   ✗ CANCEL

offline settings

After you turn on offline access, you can use this computer when it's not connected to a network.

◉ Turn on offline access
◉ Turn off offline access

When you get into Options, there are other settings you can make.

options

account

organize email

groups

site mailboxes

settings

phone

block or allow

apps

my account   connected accounts

General

Display name: michael yu
User ID: michael@ExamREVIEW.onmicrosoft.com

Mailbox Usage

76.76 KB used. At 49.5 GB you won't be able to send mail.

contact numbers

Work phone:
Mobile phone: +252 2436813

Settings for POP or IMAP access...

Edit information...

You can see the storage you have consumed so far. When you delete a message, the message will stay in the Deleted Items folder, which will still count towards the mailbox limit. When you exceed your limit you will be blocked from sending/receiving messages.

By reviewing the settings for POP or IMAP access, you can setup your own local client to retrieve emails from your Office 365 account. It gives you the server URLs, ports and encryption methods.

Use the information on this page if you need to use POP or IMAP to connect to your mailbox.

POP setting

Server name: outlook.office365.com
Port: 995
Encryption method: SSL

IMAP setting

Server name: outlook.office365.com
Port: 993
Encryption method: SSL

SMTP setting

Server name: smtp.office365.com
Port: 587
Encryption method: TLS

A site mailbox is for storing and organizing team email. The permission to use it is dictated by adding users to specific groups on your SharePoint site. You can use Outlook 2013 or OWA to access it if you have a license for SharePoint and also Exchange in your Office 365 subscription (the site email address itself does not need any Exchange license though). Email sent from this mailbox will have a From address of the sender. To use the site mailbox email address instead the Send As permission will be required.

To add a site mailbox you need to add the Site Mailbox app to the Site contents. To remove a site mailbox you need to remove the Site Mailbox app from there.

Organize email allows you to setup rules and policies.

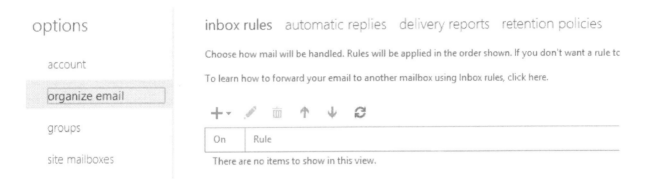

The types of inbox rules are pretty self-explanatory.

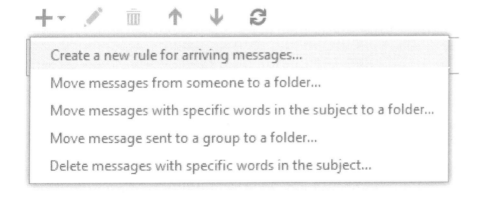

Retention policies deal with how long you want to keep your messages. These are the defaults:

Name	▲	Retention action	Retention period
1 Month Delete		Delete	30 days
1 Week Delete		Delete	7 days
Never Delete		Delete	Unlimited

To deal with junk emails, use Block or allow.

block or allow

◎ Don't move email to my Junk Email folder

◉ Automatically filter junk email

safe senders and recipients

Don't move email from these senders or domains to my Junk Email folder.

🖊 —

enter a sender or domain here   +

☐ Trust email from my contacts

blocked senders

Messaging limits

There are limits applied to every email. **As of the time of this writing:** the max total size including header and attachment is 25MB. Max 125 attachments allowed. The max number of forwarded emails per message is 30, while the max number of recipients allowed per message is 500. The max number of email that can be sent from a single client per minute is 30, while the max number of recipients that can receive emails from a single source is 10000 per day. Note that these limits cannot be changed. Again, these limits are effective as of the time of this writing. They may be subject to change!

Collaboration and SharePoint Online

You click on collaboration to access the Work Better Together section.

Work better together

Learn how to customize any team site and get the most out of SkyDrive Pro.

✓ 1   Check out SkyDrive Pro and team sites
SkyDrive Pro and Sites are always available at the top of the page.

2   Get to know SkyDrive Pro
Learn how it works: Upload, share, edit, and sync documents from any device.

3   Customize the look and feel of your team site
Reflect your professional style and brand with just a few clicks.

4   Put your site to work for the team
Add apps to help you manage tasks, schedules, and status all in one place.

In fact, collaboration can be achieved via SkyDrive Pro, Team Site and Newsfeed. SkyDrive Pro is for storage, Team Site is for collaboration, and Newsfeed is for status tracking.

Teamsite is not the same as public site. A public site is a hosted site facing the internet - you can have it customized via a web browser. An Internet Publishing Site provides even fancier features such as content management and commerce capabilities. It is, however, available only if you use SharePoint Server 2013 locally. Team site is for internal groupwork. Both can be created in the small business offering.

To be precise, the Team site as well as those sites created under it would be available only to the invited users. You need a team site for your coworkers to collaborate on documents and other files. After a new user is added to Office 365, you may add that user to the Team Site and fine tune his permissions. The relevant permission levels and group membership can be specified via Site Settings.

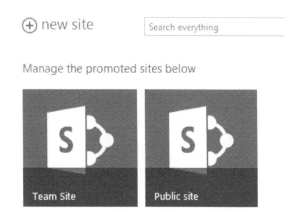

There are many different options for team site.

ExamREVIEW Team Site

Get started with your site   REMOVE THIS

| Share your site. | Working on a deadline? | Add lists, libraries, and other apps. | What's your style? | Your site. Your brand. | Keep email in context. |

Documents

⊕ new document or drag files here

✓ ☐ Name   Modified   Modified By

There are no documents in this view.

You use Share your site to invite other people to your site. This is in fact a quick way to grant permissions to people who need to use your site and encourage collaboration. If you want to share with someone outside, you may share the entire site or individual documents by inviting those users to sign in via a MS account or Office 365 user ID. Or you may send those users a guest link for them to view your documents anonymously. If you want to share a site and restrict some users from gaining access, create a subsite and set unique permissions solely for external sharing.

Share 'ExamREVIEW Team Site'   ✕

👥 Shared with lots of people

Invite people to 'Edit'

| kennethyu x   kevin yu x |

| hi |

SHOW OPTIONS

[Share] [Cancel]

There are different permission options available. As can be seen, they are pretty straight forward.

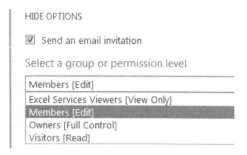

You should not assign permissions directly to individual users. You should first assign permissions to groups, then assign the users to the appropriate groups. By default, Owners have Full control, Visitors have Read, and Members have Contribute.

You may also add apps, links and libraries to your site:

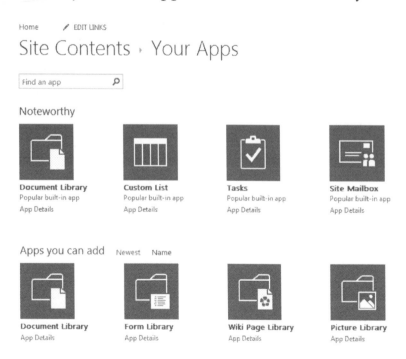

Style deals with the look of the site.

Site Settings › Change the look

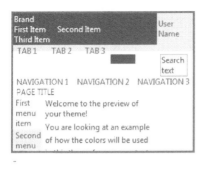
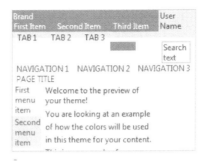

SharePoint site settings

A site collection is a hierarchical site structure made up of one top-level site plus the sites below it. Those sites in a collection have shared administration settings, common navigation plus some other common features. To be precise, a site collection can be identified by the URL of the top-level site for this site collection. Each site collection has a top-level site and may have one or more subsites. It can also possess a shared navigation structure, typically as a hierarchy. A subsite itself is a complete Web site, just that it is stored in a named subdirectory of another Web site. Its parent can be a top-level site of a site collection or simply another subsite. It is also called a subweb.

The site setting sections includes all the necessary configuration items you need to know for the exam.

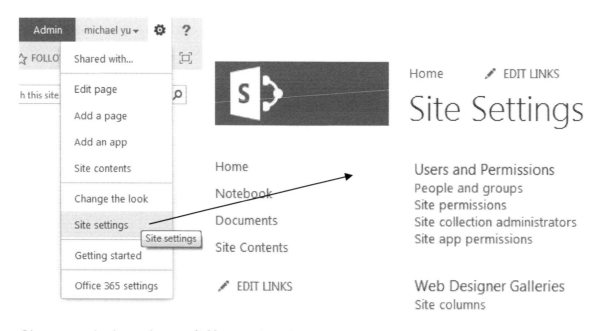

Site permissions have different levels.

Permissions are inherited. The permissions you configure for a site will affect the list, library, folder, and item in that site. To be precise, permissions correspond to 3 categories of content, which are list permissions, site permissions, and personal permissions.

Every permission level includes a combination of permissions. There are some default permission levels available:

● Full Control is by default assigned to the Owners group.

● Design is for creating lists and document libraries as well as other styling of the site.

● Edit is for editing list items and documents, and is assigned to the Members group by default.

● Contribute can view, add, update, and delete list items as well as documents.

● Read can read, add, edit, and delete existing items in existing lists and document libraries.

● Limited Access is for giving access to a single item in a list or library only. You just can't assign this permission level directly to any user or group.

● Approve can edit and approve things like pages, list items, documents…etc. By default there is an Approvers group with this permission.

● Manage Hierarchy is by default assigned to the Hierarchy Managers group.

● Restricted Read is for viewing pages and documents only.

● View Only is for viewing pages, items, and documents only (no download allowed).

Permissions › Permission Levels ⓘ

📋 Add a Permission Level | ✗ Delete Selected Permission Levels

	Permission Level	Description
☐	Full Control	Has full control.
☑	Design	Can view, add, update, delete, approve, and customize.
☑	Edit	Can add, edit and delete lists; can view, add, update and delete list items and documents.
☑	Contribute	Can view, add, update, and delete list items and documents.
☑	Read	Can view pages and list items and download documents.
☐	Limited Access	Can view specific lists, document libraries, list items, folders, or documents when given per
☑	View Only	Can view pages, list items, and documents. Document types with server-side file handlers (downloaded.
☑	Create new subsites	Can create new subsites

You can delete a permission level. You can also click Add a permission level to make a custom one. In fact, instead of changing a default permission level, it is a better idea to create a new custom one.

Permission Levels › Add a Permission Level

Name and Description

Type a name and description for your permission level. The name is shown on the permissions page. The name and description are shown on the add users page.

Name:

[   ]

Description:

[   ]

Permissions

Choose which permissions to include in this permission level. Use the **Select All** check box to select or clear all permissions.

Select the permissions to include in this permission level.

☐ **Select All**

List Permissions

☐ Manage Lists - Create and delete lists, add or remove cc

☐ Override List Behaviors - Discard or check in a document settings which allow users to read/edit only their own item

☐ Add Items - Add items to lists and add documents to do

☐ Edit Items - Edit items in lists, edit documents in documei

Name:

> custompermission

Description:

> this is a test custom permission.

Select the permissions to include in this permission level.

☐ **Select All**

List Permissions

☑ Manage Lists - Create and delete lists, add or remove columns in a list, and add

☐ Override List Behaviors - Discard or check in a document which is checked out to
settings which allow users to read/edit only their own items

☑ Add Items - Add items to lists and add documents to document libraries.

You can even copy the permission level that matches your requirement and then make additional changes (by selecting the permissions to include) accordingly – you click to go into a particular permission level, then scroll to the bottom of the screen and click Copy Permission Level.

Personal Permissions

☑ Manage Personal Views - Create, change, and delete personal views of lists.

☑ Add/Remove Personal Web Parts - Add or remove personal Web Parts on a Web Part Page.

☑ Update Personal Web Parts - Update Web Parts to display personalized information.

———————————————▶   [Copy Permission Level]   [Submit]

SharePoint permissions that depend on other permissions have dependency involved. At the time you select a permission that depends on another, the associated permission(s) will be automatically chosen. The only permission that requires no dependency is Open. In fact all other permissions depend on Open in order to operate as expected.

Access request is a feature that allows other people to request access to contents that they don't have permission to access. A site owner can enable this feature so that someone may request access to his site via email.

SharePoint groups

A SharePoint group has users who share the same permission level. By default, each SharePoint site has its own SharePoint groups assigned. You can create a new group by clicking on Create Group. You become the owner of this group automatically.

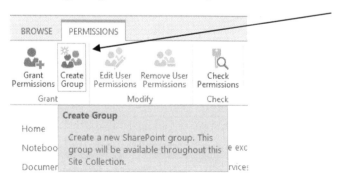

People and Groups ▸ Create Group ⓘ

Name and About Me Description

Type a name and description for the group.

Name:

About Me:

Click for help about adding HTML formatting.

Owner

The owner can change anything about the group such as adding and removing members or deleting the group. Only one user or group can be the owner.

Group owner:

michael yu x

Group Settings

Specify who has permission to see the list of group members and who has permission to add and remove members from the group.

Who can view the membership of the group?

⦿ Group Members

Who can edit the membership of the group?

⦿ Group Owner

You can make the necessary permission settings at the time of group creation:

Choose the permission level group members get on this site: https://examreview.sharepoint.com

- ☐ Full Control - Has full control.
- ☐ Design - Can view, add, update, delete, approve, and customize.
- ☐ Edit - Can add, edit and delete lists; can view, add, update and delete list items and documents.
- ☐ Contribute - Can view, add, update, and delete list items and documents.
- ☐ Read - Can view pages and list items and download documents.
- ☐ View Only - Can view pages, list items, and documents. Document types with server-side file handlers can be viewed in the browser but not downloaded.
- ☐ Create new subsites - Can create new subsites

Site features and other settings

The Site Administration has the following sections:

- Regional settings

- Language settings

- Site libraries and lists – it allows you to add apps, libraries and lists. You can also create subsite.

- User alerts – it allows you to display and delete user alerts

- RSS

- Sites and workspaces – you create site and/or workspace from here.

- Workflow settings

- Term store management

Site Settings ▸ Sites and Workspaces ⓘ

🖳 Create | Site Creation Permissions

Sites   Description
There are no Sites. To create one, click Create above.

Document Workspaces
There are no Document Workspaces. To create one, click Create above.

Meeting Workspaces
There are no Meeting Workspaces. To create one, click Create above.

Site Contents › New SharePoint Site

Title and Description

Title:

testsite

Description:

this is a test site

Web Site Address

URL name:

https://examreview-my.sharepoint.com/personal/mich.../ testsite

Template Selection

Select a language:

English

Select a template:

| Collaboration | Enterprise | Duet Enterprise |

Team Site
Blog
Project Site

When you create a site, you can have your creation based on a template. In terms of permission, you may inherit permissions from parent or create unique permissions.

Permissions

You can give permission to access your new site to the same users who have access to this parent site, or you can give permission to a unique set of users.

Note: If you select **Use same permissions as parent site**, one set of user permissions is shared by both sites. Consequently, you cannot change user permissions on your new site unless you are an administrator of this parent site.

User Permissions:

◉ Use same permissions as parent site
○ Use unique permissions

Navigation

Display this site on the top link bar of the parent site?

◉ Yes   ○ No

Navigation Inheritance

Use the top link bar from the parent site?

○ Yes   ◉ No

After site creation you can click Share your site to invite people to use it.

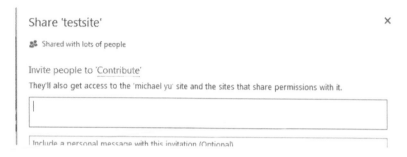

Share 'testsite'   ×

👥 Shared with lots of people

Invite people to 'Contribute'
They'll also get access to the 'michael yu' site and the sites that share permissions with it.

Include a personal message with this invitation (Optional)

You may create a subsite if necessary.

Site Contents

Lists, Libraries, and other Apps

add an app

Documents
1 item
Modified 3 days ago

MicroFeed
2 items
Modified 3 days ago

Social
3 items
Modified 3 minutes ago

Subsites

⊕ new subsite   ⟵

📄 testsite   Modified 3 minutes ago

Site Contents › New SharePoint Site

You may then share the subsite and drag files to it.

Do note that many of the site settings cannot be performed directly on the subsite. Instead you need to make the settings on the parent site.

Site Actions
Manage site features
Reset to site definition
Delete this site

Site Collection Administration
Go to top level site settings ⟵

Regional Settings deals with locale, timezone, calendar and workweek settings.

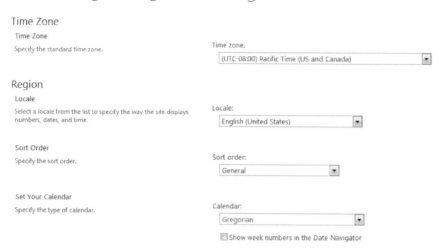

Language Settings allows you to pick alternate languages (users can switch languages at wish). The default language was set at the time of site creation and is not changeable.

Site Settings ▸ Language Settings

Default Language

The default language of the site is specified when the site is first created.

Default Language:

English

Alternate language(s)

Specify the alternate language(s) that this site will support. Users navigating to this site will be able to change the display language of the site to any one of these languages.

Alternate language(s):

☐ Arabic

☐ Bulgarian

☐ Catalan

☐ Chinese (Traditional)

Do note that both regional settings and site settings are site-specific. With Overwrite Translations, the user-specified text may be translated into the alternate languages chosen. This option is for determining whether it should automatically overwrite the existing translations made.

The Term Store Management Tool can be used to configure managed metadata for your sites. This is all about implementing formal taxonomies through managed terms (for the sake of maintaining consistency of metadata throughout all of your contents). You can even import from a term set file.

 Site Settings › Term Store Management Tool

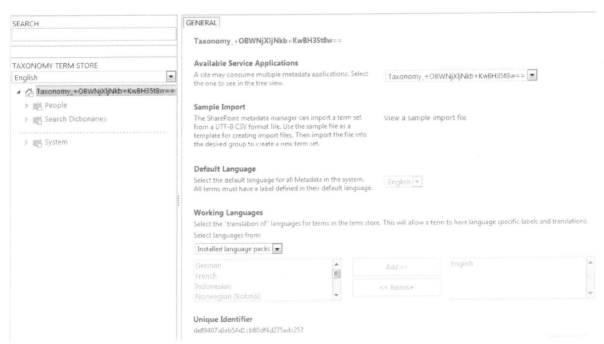

The term set file is a CSV file which can be viewed through Excel.

A	B	C	D	E	F	G	H	I	J	K	L
Term Set N	Term Set D	LCID	Available f	Term Desc	Level 1 Te	Level 2 Te	Level 3 Te	Level 4 Te	Level 5 Te	Level 6 Te	Level 7 Term
Political Ge	A sample term set, des		TRUE	One of the	Continent						
			TRUE	Entity defir	Continent	Political Entity					
			TRUE	Politically (	Continent	Political En	Country				
			TRUE	Administra	Continent	Political En	Country	Province or	State		
			TRUE	Large sub-(	Continent	Political En	Country	Province or	County or	Region	
			TRUE	Small villag	Continent	Political En	Country	Province or	County or	Hamlet	
			TRUE	Collection (	Continent	Political En	Country	Province or	County or	Village	
			TRUE	A small cit	Continent	Political En	Country	Province or	County or	Town	
			TRUE	An incorpc	Continent	Political En	Country	Province or	County or	City	
			TRUE	A division	Continent	Political En	Country	Province or	County or	City	District
			TRUE	A sub-secti	Continent	Political En	Country	Province or	County or	City	Borough
			TRUE	Unofficial (	Continent	Political En	Country	Province or	County or	City	Neighborhood

A Managed Metadata column refers to a new column type that you may add to lists, libraries, or other content types so that your site users may pick values from a specific set of managed terms.

On the other hand, Site Collection Administration has these links:

- Recycle bin

- Search Result Sources

- Search Result Types

- Search Query Rules

- Search Schema

- Search Settings

- Search Configuration Import

- Search Configuration Export

- Site collection features

- Site hierarchy

- Site collection audit settings

- Portal site connection

- Storage Metrics

- Site collection app permissions

- Content type publishing

- HTML Field Security

- Help settings

- SharePoint Designer Settings

- Site collection health checks

- Site collection upgrade

When your users delete things, the things deleted are first placed in the Recycle Bin. You may view and manage these deleted items via Recycle Bin page. There are 2 levels - first there is the user's Recycle Bin, then there is the Site Collection Recycle Bin.

Site Settings › Recycle Bin ⓘ

⤺Restore Selection | ✖ Delete Selection | 🗑 Empty Recycle Bin

☐	Type	Name	Original Location	Deleted By

There are no items in the recycle bin.

You may restore items in the end user Recycle Bin via the End user Recycle Bin items view. Or you may restore items in the Site Collection Recycle Bin via the Deleted from end user Recycle Bin view. The latest retention period announced is 90 days.

Site hierarchy lists all the available sites and subsites.

Site Settings ‣ Site Hierarchy ⓘ

Site URL	Title
https://examreview-my.sharepoint.com/personal/michael_examreview_onmicrosoft_com/testsite	testsite
https://examreview-my.sharepoint.com/personal/michael_examreview_onmicrosoft_com/testsubsite	test sub site

Site collection features is for activating/deactivating individual features.

Site Settings ‣ Site Collection Features

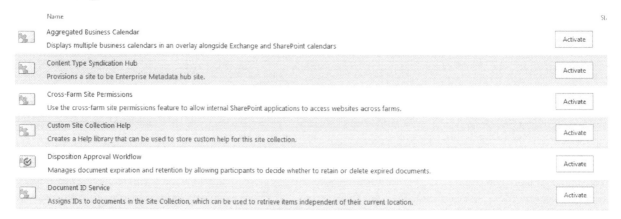

Storage Metrics tells the current quotas.

Site Settings › Storage Metrics ⓘ

Site Collection

Type	Name	Total Size↓	% of Parent		% of Site Quota	
📄	Highlights.aspx	7.8 KB	100.00 %		0.00 %	
📄	blog.xsl	5.5 KB	100.00 %		0.00 %	
📄	default.aspx	5.2 KB	100.00 %		0.00 %	
📄	newsfeed.aspx	4.9 KB	100.00 %		0.00 %	
📄	RecentlyAssigned.aspx	4.8 KB	100.00 %		0.00 %	
📄	AllTasks.aspx	4.8 KB	100.00 %		0.00 %	
📄	CompletedTasks.aspx	4.8 KB	100.00 %		0.00 %	
📄	EditTask.aspx	4.6 KB	100.00 %		0.00 %	

If you subscribe to these plans you can have max 10000 site collections: E1, E3, E4, A1, A3, A4, G1, G3, G4. The publishing error log can be obtained through Content Type Publishing. In SharePoint Online, there are two types of log related to publishing. The Content type service application error log is available on hub sites for content type publishing. It is for capturing publishing error information for the subscriber sites. The Content type publishing error log is different - it captures publishing error information for a particular site.

Content Type Publishing Hubs

Refresh All Published Content Types

The next time the content type subscriber timer job runs, update all published content types.

☐ Refresh all published content types on next update

Content type publishing error log

Content type publishing error log contains errors that happened during content type syndication for this site.

Content type publishing error log

Hubs

These service applications are publishing content types to this site collection. In order to edit content types that have been published from these locations or to create and publish a new content type, select the hub URL. To view the subscribed content type on this site collection, select the content type.

Taxonomy_+OBWNjXIjNkb+KwBH35t8w==
No hub defined

When a site collection has files customized, they may not work properly during an upgrade. By running a health check you may view a health check report or even reset the files to the default values.

Talking about site collection upgrades, there are several options available.

Site Settings ‣ Site Collection Upgrade

Check on the current upgrade status or get a copy of your upgrade logs. If upgrade has failed on your site collection, you can try to resume upgrade.

REVIEW SITE COLLECTION UPGRADE STATUS

You may "Allow creation of old version site collections, but prevent creation of new version site collections". You may also "Allow creation of old version site collections, and creation of new version site collections." And you may "Prevent creation of old version site collections, but allow creation of new version site collections." Their meanings are very straight forward.

Apps for mobile devices

Office 365 supports a wide range of mobile devices. From the phone & tablet section you can select a mobile platform and then choose the apps to install.

Choose your phone or tablet

Phone	Tablet
Windows Phone	Windows 8 tablet
iPhone	Windows RT device
Android Phone	iPad
BlackBerry®	
Nokia (Symbian OS)	
Other	

Choose your phone or tablet

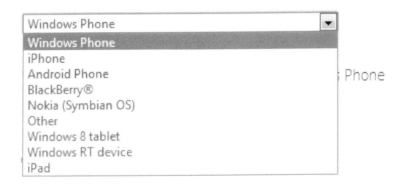

Windows Phone

Windows Phone
iPhone
Android Phone
BlackBerry®
Nokia (Symbian OS)
Other
Windows 8 tablet
Windows RT device
iPad

Phone

Get other apps

Lync   SharePoint

Get the apps

OneNote
Organize your notes and
share them.

get app ←

Lync
Send instant message
and make calls.

get app ←

Lync Online

Lync provides voice mail and instant messaging. It works with Exchange to provide unified messaging. Lync 2013 comes with the Office Pro Plus, which can be installed along with your subscription (when you install Lync, your computer will be automatically configured for accommodating the necessary network traffics). Or you may use the web based scheduler without installing the local client:

Lync

Install Lync

Lync 2013 is included in the latest version of Office.

Lync

Install the latest version of Office

Launch Lync Web Scheduler

If you don't have Outlook or Windows, use Lync Web Scheduler to set up, join, and manage Lync meetings. Learn more

Launch Lync Web Scheduler

MS has a summary of all the Lync settings available at:

http://onlinehelp.microsoft.com/en-us/office365-enterprises/hh416768.aspx

License restrictions, on the other hand, can be found here (audio and video are not available in some countries):

http://office.microsoft.com/en-us/business/microsoft-office-license-restrictions-FX103037529.aspx?redir=0

About license restrictions

Office 365 is available for purchase by customers located in the following countries/regions: Algeria, Arc Belarus, Belgium, Brazil, Bulgaria, Canada, Chile, China, Colombia, Costa Rica, Croatia, Cyprus, Czech Rep Egypt, El Salvador, Estonia, Finland, France, Germany, Greece, Guatemala, Hong Kong SAR, Hungary, Ice Jordan, Kazakhstan, Kenya, Republic of Korea, Kuwait, Latvia, Liechtenstein, Lithuania, Luxembourg, forn Malta, Mexico, Montenegro, Morocco, Netherlands, New Zealand, Nigeria, Norway, Oman, Pakistan, Par Portugal, Puerto Rico, Qatar, Romania, Russia, Saudi Arabia, Serbia, Singapore, Slovakia, Slovenia, South Taiwan, Thailand, Trinidad and Tobago, Tunisia, Turkey, Ukraine, United Arab Emirates, United Kingdom,

Customers that purchase Office 365 may assign an Office 365 license to a user that resides anywhere ir People's Republic of Korea, Sudan, and Syria. Please note that the availability of features for these users the countries where certain Office 365 features may be unavailable to licensed users:

Country	Lync Online	Exchange Online	SharePoint Online
Albania	No Audio/Video	No Hosted Voicemail	No restrictions
Bangladesh	No Audio/Video	No Hosted Voicemail	No restrictions
Brunei	No Audio/Video	No Hosted Voicemail	No restrictions

For Lync to work, you need to configure your network so your external firewall can accommodate Lync traffics. If you are using your own domain for Lync, you must add the corresponding records (both CNAME and SRV) to the external DNS server. When external SRV queries are not allowed, you will also need to add records to the internal DNS server. All these records should be configured with a Time-To-Live of 1 hour.

The external firewalls (or reverse proxy) should have these outbound ports opened:

- 443

- 3478

- 5223

- 50000-50019

- 50020-50039

- 50040-50059

Outgoing TLS and HTTPs traffics should be allowed to these locations:

- *.online.lync.com

- *.onmicrosoft.com

- *.infra.lync.com

- *.lync.com

MS also publishes the IP addresses used by Lync Online. These addresses can be found here: http://technet.microsoft.com/en-us/library/hh372948.aspx

Lync Online URLs and IP Address Ranges

9 out of 13 rated this helpful - Rate this topic

Topic Last Modified: 2013-04-10

Following are the lists of IP ranges and URLs used by the Lync Online service. Your corporate network must allc

> ◆ **Important:**
>
> For a complete list of Office 365 routing requirements, see Office 365 URLs and IP address ranges at http://gc
> For firewall port and protocol settings, see http://go.microsoft.com/fwlink/p/?LinkId=282684.

IP Ranges

```
65.54.54.128/25
65.55.121.128/27
65.55.127.0/24
111.221.17.128/27
```

To test connectivity for Lync, use the Remote Connectivity Analyzer web based tool available at https://www.testexchangeconnectivity.com/.

Lync-to-phone is a special feature available only in Lync Plan 3. With it, you can set up an account with a service provider so that Lync users may make calls to or receive calls from any regular phone number. One way to set up Lync-to-phone voice mail is by enabling users for the Exchange Online feature known as Unified Messaging. This feature requires Exchange Plan 2 though. FYI, in Exchange Online the Enable-UMMailbox cmdlet can be used to turn on Unified Messaging for the mail-enabled users.

There is a Public IM connectivity setting which controls IM and audio/video communication with contacts using Skype. This feature is enabled by default. For it to work properly, you need to set up domain federation. In fact, if you disable federation you will also disable public IM connectivity.

Domain federation is required (and must be setup on both sides to communicate using the same feature) so that your own Lync Online users can communicate with other organizations that use Lync or Skype. You may choose to federate only with the domains you specify, or to domains that are not blocked.

Presence privacy mode is a feature for setting Lync presence. Automatically display presence information is the default. With it, anyone other than those in the External or Blocked privacy relationship groups may view the presence status. Display presence information only to a user's contacts is another. With it, only those in the contact list that are not External nor Blocked may view their presence status. Do note that it is possible for individual users to override this setting via the Lync options dialog box.

Special Topic: Exchange ECP

Depending on the plan you subscribe to, you may have access to the Exchange Control Panel ECP (aka EAC). MS deliberately hides ECP in the small business plan - you need to use a special URL to access it:

https://<PodNumber>.outlook.com/ecp

OR
https://outlook.office365.com/ecp/?realm=examreview.onmicrosoft.com#modurl=0&path=/mail (replace examreview.onmicrosoft.com with your own).

There are some key features available in the ECP. You can perform batch migration (TO and FROM Exchange Online):

These are the migration types available:

Exchange Server 2013 first introduces batch moves and migration endpoints. Migration endpoints are management objects representing remote server and connections. Batch move uses the Mailbox Replication service MRS to move multiple mailboxes in large batches with email notification, automatic retry and automatic prioritization. This is NOT available in Exchange 2010. Cross-forest move involves moving mailboxes between two on-premises Exchange forests. It has to make use of a RemoteMove endpoint. Remote move is for hybrid deployment - it involves onboarding or offboarding migrations (ie. moves mailboxes between an on-premises organization and Office 365). The New-MigrationEndpoint cmdlet can be used to configure the necessary connection settings. Set-MigrationConfig is for editing the migration configurations. Set-MigrationEndpoint is for making settings on the migration endpoint.

Permissions allows you to configure the various admin/user roles and OWA policies. Note that a default role assignment policy (in User Roles) deals with the granting of permissions to the end users to perform self admin tasks.

admin roles   user roles   Outlook Web App policies

Protection provides all sorts of filters and spam protection …etc. These filters are by default enabled. The quarantine is also here so you can selectively release messages.

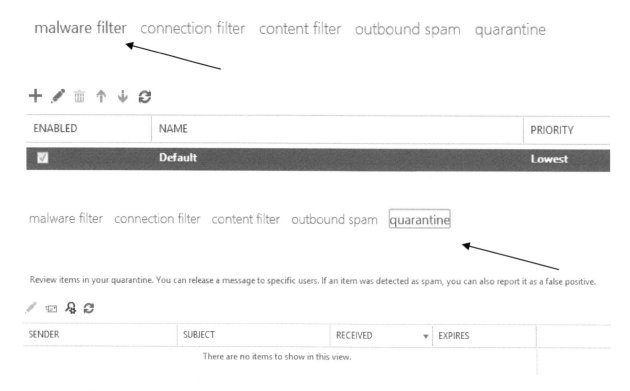

Mail flow is for configuring delivery reports, message trace, accepted domains and connectors, while Organization is dealing with sharing and apps.

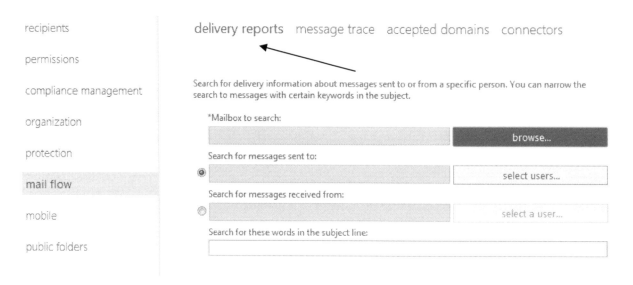

Message trace can be performed based on time, sender, receiver, message ID…etc.

delivery reports message trace accepted domains connectors

Search for email messages from or to a user or users. You can specify user names or fully qualified email addresses. Wildcards are supported.

Sender:

[   ] [add users...]

Recipient:

[   ] [add users...]

Message was sent or received:

[Last 48 hours   ▼]

Delivery status:

[▼]

Message ID:

[   ]

It is possible to setup a Public folder, but you need to first setup a public folder mailbox.

recipients

permissions

compliance management

organization

protection

mail flow

mobile

public folders

public folders   public folder mailboxes

+ ✎ 🗑 ↑ ⟳ ...

[\   ▶]

SUBFOLDER NAME	▲	HAS SUBFOLDERS	MAIL ENABLED

No public folders exist in this organization. Before you create a public folder, please make sure that you created at least one public folder mailbox. To create a public folder, click 'Add' +. After you create the public folder, you'll need to assign permissions so users can access it and create subfolders.

Review Questions:

1. Describe Active Directory.

2. What is Windows Azure?

3. Describe Active Directory Federation Services.

4. What is Windows Intune?

5. ActiveSync is for synchronizing:

6. Single sign-on SSO refers to:

7. What is OnRamp for?

8. Dial-in conferencing is a feature that allows:

9. Talking about conferencing, presence statuses may include:

10. Describe Outlook Web App.

11. What does community participation allow?

12. In terms of groups, note that under the Site settings of SharePoint online there are 4 groups by default, which are:

13. "Company Administrator" includes:

14. "Everyone" includes everyone but:

15. Site Collection Administrators is a group with full control over:

16. Office 365 has several different types of administrator roles as defined by MS, including:

17. Compare full administration with limited administration.

18. What are roles?

19. How do you perform bulk importing of users?

20. To avoid code issue you should save a CSV file in what format?

21. Assigning license is a necessary step because:

22. When a new user first logins, he will be asked to set a new password, which must be a strong password with at least __ characters but no more than ___.

23. A common shared mailbox can be used for what purpose?

24. In the context of Outlook, a shared mailbox is in a sense a form of:

25. External contacts represent:

26. With the Office 365 Small Business Premium offering, each user can install the latest version of Office on max _____ computers.

27. Exchange Online requires what DNS records to operate?

28. Lync Online requires what DNS records to operate?

29. Office 365 supports which Outlook client versions?

30. Describe Workflow.

31. Talking about Current status, Investigating means:

32. Talking about Current status, Restoring service means:

33. Talking about Current status, Extended recovery means:

34. SkyDrive Pro is supposed to serve as a replacement for:

35. By default SkyDrive Pro offers a ____GB storage with a max upload size of __ GB.

36. With the Windows Azure Active Directory Sync tool Configuration Wizard, a _____ account will be created in your local forest.

37. By default recurring directory synchronizations will take place every ____ hours.

38. By default you can't synchronize more than _____ directory objects.

39. Keep in mind, the computer performing directory synchronization must run which OS minimum?

40. When the synchronization process creates mail-enabled users in Office 365, the same user principal name UPN will be used together with the passwords. True?

41. To connect to the online service via the PowerShell, run_____ To seek help on a cmdlet, use _____.

42. Each time you start Windows PowerShell you are only in the server session. True?

43. You use _____ to retrieve either an individual user or a list of users.

44. You use _____ to update a user object.

45. You use _____ to add members to a group, or use _____ to retrieve a group.

46. _____ can be used to create a new group.

47. You use _____ to add a user (not a group) to a role.

48. You use _____ to retrieve a list of admin roles, or use _____ to retrieve all the admin roles that a specified user is belonging to.

49. You use _____ to find out about all the subscriptions you have purchased.

50. _____ shows all the SKUs you own.

51. You use _____ to switch on or off directory synchronization.

52. You use _____ to retrieve a contact, or use _____ to delete one.

53. When migrating Exchange users you should require them to change their password via the _____ attribute.

54. When should you deploy Exchange via hybrid deployment?

55. What are distribution groups?

56. There are limits applied to every email. The max total size including header and attachment is ___MB. Max ___ attachments allowed.

57. What is a site collection?

58. What is a subsite?

59. Permissions correspond to 3 categories of content, which are:

60. What is a SharePoint group?

61. The Term Store Management Tool can be used to configure:

62. A Managed Metadata column refers to:

63. When your users delete things, the things deleted are first placed in:

64. The default retention period of Recycle Bin is _____ days.

65. If you are using your own DNS domain for Lync, you must:

66. What tool can you use to test connectivity for Lync?

67. Lync-to-phone is a special feature for:

68. One way to set up Lync-to-phone voice mail is by enabling:

69. In Exchange Online the _____ cmdlet can be used to turn on Unified Messaging for the mail-enabled users.

70. What is the default for the Presence privacy mode?

71. Public IM connectivity is for controlling:

72. Domain federation is required for what purpose?

73. A site mailbox is for:

74. The permission to use a site mailbox is dictated by:

75. Email sent from a site mailbox will have a From address of:

76. It is possible to setup a Public folder, but you need to first setup a:

77. Describe Batch Move.

78. Describe Cross-forest Move.

Answers:

1. *Active Directory AD stores information of all network objects and makes the information easy to find. It is a logical and hierarchical presentation and storage of shared resources such as servers, volumes, printers...etc.*

2. *Windows Azure is in fact a cloud implementation of AD.*

3. *Active Directory Federation Services ADFS provides Web single-sign-on SSO for authenticating web user to multiple Web applications.*

4. *Windows Intune is a cloud-based client management solution.*

5. *ActiveSync is for synchronizing email messages, calendar, and contacts lists in the Exchange Server mailbox with a Windows Mobile powered device (such as Windows Phone).*

6. *Single sign-on SSO refers to the kind of access control method which enables a user to authenticate once and gain access to network resources of other software systems.*

7. *You use the Office 365 Deployment Readiness Tool (OnRamp) to evaluate readiness for Office 365.*

8. *Dial-in conferencing allows phone access to online meetings for those having no access to computer.*

9. *Talking about conferencing, presence statuses may include Available, Busy, Away, and Do Not Disturb. In fact, the status is based on Outlook Calendar or other Lync activities.*

10. *OWA Outlook Web App is a native app for iPhone and iPad. It allows mobile devices to work and sync with Outlook. Simply put, it works almost the same way that Outlook Web Access does in a PC based browser (and with some additional features).*

11. *When community participation is turned on, users who browse the Office 365 community can post questions and comments to the forums using either an Office 365 user ID or a MS account.*

12. *In terms of groups, note that under the Site settings of SharePoint online there are 4 groups by default, which are members, visitors, owners and Excel Services viewers.*

13. *Company Administrator covers all Office 365 admins, including the Global and Billing admins.*

14. *Everyone includes also the external users.*

15. *Site Collection Administrators is a group with full control over all SharePoint sites in the site collection. By default all company admins belong to this group.*

16. *Office 365 has several different types of administrator roles as defined by MS, including Billing admin (available in Office 365 for enterprises only since billing changes cannot be made in other offerings), global admin (which is you if you are the one who signed up and bought Office 365), password admin, service admin, and user management admin.*

17. *Full administration possesses privileges equivalent to those of global administrator. Limited administration possesses privileges equivalent to those of password administrator.*

18. *Roles can be thought of as collections of permissions to use resources appropriate to a staff's job function. This works with the assumption that all permissions needed to perform a job function can be neatly encapsulated.*

19. *Bulk importing users is not possible via the portal as of the time of this writing. You need to prepare a CSV file and use the Powershell to do the job.*

20. *To avoid code issue you should save the CSV file in a Unicode or UTF-8 format.*

21. *Assigning license is a necessary step if you want a new user to be able to actually use Office 365. When you create a new user account, a license should be associated with the user so he can access the Office 365 services.*

22. *When a new user first logins, he will be asked to set a new password, which must be a strong password with at least 8 characters but no more than 16 (this password should have lowercase and uppercase characters plus numbers or symbols).*

23. *A common shared mailbox can be used by multiple users to send and receive emails. You can add multiple users to it. According to MS, a common mailbox is a great way for handling customer queries.*

24. *In the context of Outlook, a shared mailbox is in a sense a form of Delegate Access.*

25. *External contacts represent those email recipients who are NOT inside your organization (they have e-mail addresses that do not belong to your domain nor your organization - they just don't have a mailbox in your environment). These contacts can be added as a shared contact.*

26. *With the Office 365 Small Business Premium offering, each user can install the latest version of Office on max 5 computers (compatible with PCs or Macs).*

27. *Exchange Online requires a MX record for email routing, a CNAME record that help users to set up a connection via autodiscovery, and a TXT/SPF record which allows outlook.com to send email on behalf of your own domain.*

28. *Lync Online also requires some DNS records. It needs some SRV records to support instant messaging, presence, and meeting sign-in. It also needs CNAME records for autodiscovery by desktop and mobile clients.*

29. *Office 365 supports Outlook 2007, 2010 and 2013. However, they may not be installed on the same computer simultaneously.*

30. *Workflow is in fact a feature of SharePoint – workflows are pre-programmed for automating business processes. Do note that SharePoint Online can only support sandboxed solutions, that all code-based workflows are not allowed to run at all.*

31. *Current status is for tracking service health. Investigating means there is a potential service incident currently under investigation.*

32. *Current status is for tracking service health. Restoring service means the service problem is being resolved.*

33. *Current status is for tracking service health. Extended recovery means it is going to take some time for the service to be normal again.*

34. *SkyDrive Pro is a cloud based storage drive. You can keep your stuff private until you share them. It is supposed to serve as a replacement for My Documents.*

35. *By default SkyDrive Pro offers a 25GB storage with a max upload size of 2GB.*

36. *With the Windows Azure Active Directory Sync tool Configuration Wizard, a MSOL_AD_SYNC account will be created in your local forest. This is a service account that will be used to synchronize directory information.*

37. *By default recurring directory synchronizations will take place every 3 hours.*

38. *By default you can't synchronize more than 50000 directory objects.*

39. *Keep in mind, the computer performing directory synchronization must run Windows Server 2008 R2 or later (it must be a server OS), and must be joined to AD.*

40. *When the synchronization process creates mail-enabled users in Office 365, the same user principal name UPN will be used. However, passwords will NOT be synchronized by default.*

41. *To connect to the online service via the PowerShell, run connect-msolservice. To seek help on a cmdlet, use get-help <cmdlet-name> -detailed.*

42. *Each time you start Windows PowerShell you are only in the session of your local computer, which is a client-side session.*

43. *You use Get-MsolUser to retrieve either an individual user or a list of users.*

44. *You use Set-MsolUser to update a user object.*

45. *You use Add-MsolGroupMember to add members to a group, or use Get-MsolGroup to retrieve a group.*

46. *New-MsolGroup can be used to create a new group.*

47. *You use Add-MsolRoleMember to add a user (not a group) to a role.*

48. *You use Get-MsolRole to retrieve a list of admin roles, or use Get-MsolUserRole to retrieve all the admin roles that a specified user is belonging to.*

49. *You use Get-MsolSubscription to find out about all the subscriptions you have purchased.*

50. *Get-MsolAccountSku shows all the SKUs you own.*

51. *You use Set-MsolDirSyncEnabled to switch on or off directory synchronization.*

52. *You use Get-MsolContact to retrieve a contact, or use Remove-MsolContact to delete one.*

53. *When migrating Exchange users you should require them to change their password via the ForceChangePassword attribute (this is for the sake of security).*

54. *If you want to maintain mailboxes both locally and in the cloud, you should deploy Exchange via hybrid deployment. For this to work, you need to run Exchange Server 2010 or later.*

55. *Distribution groups are collections of recipients that appear in the shared address book. When an email message reaches a group, it simply goes to all members of the group.*

56. *There are limits applied to every email. As of the time of this writing: the max total size including header and attachment is 25MB. Max 125 attachments allowed.*

57. *A site collection is a hierarchical site structure made up of one top-level site plus the sites below it. Those sites in a collection have shared administration settings, common navigation plus some other common features.*

58. *Each site collection has a top-level site and may have one or more subsites. It can also possess a shared navigation structure, typically as a hierarchy. A subsite itself is a complete Web site, just that it is stored in a named subdirectory of another Web site.*

59. Permissions correspond to 3 categories of content, which are list permissions, site permissions, and personal permissions.

60. A SharePoint group has users who share the same permission level. By default, each SharePoint site has its own SharePoint groups assigned.

61. The Term Store Management Tool can be used to configure managed metadata for your sites. This is all about implementing formal taxonomies through managed terms.

62. A Managed Metadata column refers to a new column type that you may add to lists, libraries, or other content types so that your site users may pick values from a specific set of managed terms.

63. When your users delete things, the things deleted are first placed in the Recycle Bin. You may view and manage these deleted items via Recycle Bin page. There are 2 levels - first there is the user's Recycle Bin, then there is the Site Collection Recycle Bin.

64. The retention period of Recycle Bin is 90 days.

65. If you are using your own domain for Lync, you must add the corresponding records (both CNAME and SRV) to the external DNS server. When external SRV queries are not allowed, you will also need to add records to the internal DNS server.

66. To test connectivity for Lync, use the Remote Connectivity Analyzer web based tool available at https://www.testexchangeconnectivity.com/.

67. Lync-to-phone is a special feature available only in Lync Plan 3. With it, you can set up an account with a service provider so that Lync users may make calls to or receive calls from any regular phone number.

68. One way to set up Lync-to-phone voice mail is by enabling users for the Exchange Online feature known as Unified Messaging. This feature requires Exchange Plan 2 though.

69. In Exchange Online the Enable-UMMailbox cmdlet can be used to turn on Unified Messaging for the mail-enabled users.

70. *Presence privacy mode is a feature for setting Lync presence. Automatically display presence information is the default.*

71. *There is a Public IM connectivity setting which controls IM and audio/video communication with contacts using Skype. This feature is enabled by default.*

72. *Domain federation is required (and must be setup on both sides to communicate using the same feature) so that your own Lync Online users can communicate with other organizations that use Lync or Skype.*

73. *A site mailbox is for storing and organizing team email.*

74. *The permission to use a site mailbox is dictated by adding users to specific groups on your SharePoint site.*

75. *Email sent from a site mailbox will have a From address of the sender.*

76. *It is possible to setup a Public folder, but you need to first setup a public folder mailbox.*

77. *Batch move uses the Mailbox Replication service MRS to move multiple mailboxes in large batches with email notification, automatic retry and automatic prioritization.*

78. *Cross-forest move involves moving mailboxes between two on-premises Exchange forests.*

End of book